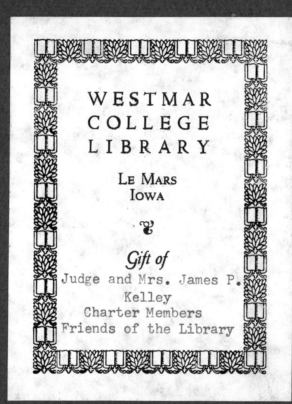

Architecture of the California Missions

ARCHITECTURE OF THE CALIFORNIA MISSIONS

text by
Kurt Baer

photographs by
Hugo Rudinger

UNIVERSITY OF CALIFORNIA PRESS

Berkeley and Los Angeles

1958

University of California Press
Berkeley and Los Angeles, California

Cambridge University Press
London, England

© 1958 by The Regents of the University of California

Library of Congress Catalog Card Number: 58–11921

Designed by Rita Carroll

Printed in the United States of America

for
Roderick

Preface

Certainly there are few buildings in the United States more picturesque and of greater interest than the missions of California. Their romantic history, the often exciting story of their founding, their golden age, their decline, and now their virtual renaissance—all this has been told many times.

Primarily this work is a study of mission architecture. It concerns itself with the interpretation of stylistic sources in the remote past of classical Rome and the Moors of Spain and in the primitive and the baroque in Mexico, and especially with these manifestations in the California buildings. The book is not intended as a history of, nor as a guide book to, the missions. It does not list the missions in the order of their founding or in geographical sequence along what was once El Camino Real. Rather, they are grouped or divided according to the architectural style best represented. The text indicates the probable origins and the four main styles into which the extant buildings can be, albeit arbitrarily, grouped. Because of renovation, reconstruction, and even restoration, in many missions the styles overlap; therefore a mission may be an example of more than one style. Although there was a basic plan common to all the missions, predicated on needs of the moment of founding, elaborations were inevitably made once the larger churches and their contiguous conventos and the mission quadrangle were constructed.

Unfortunately the available archival documents giving information on plans and detail drawings—if these ever existed—have been lost. The annual memorias and the irregular inventories as a rule indicated only what type of construction had been undertaken or completed at a mission during the preceding calendar year. Therefore, much that pertains to style, to construction, and to the decoration or embellishment of the missions must be based on assumption, on extant and available records, old photographs, and drawings, and on the examination of existing buildings. The building padres and their masons and helpers left no drawings of their plans or elevations. The earliest known sketches date from between 1840 and 1850, and not all of these are completely reliable, for too often the recorder was tempered by romanticism and thus distorted proportions or added or subtracted details, or he simply

*could not draw. Yet it is from these sketches that the appearance of the mis-
sions before they were doomed by secularization must be assumed.*

*The mission churches of California were founded and built within a very
short span of years. For two reasons their structures never reached the relative
magnificence of those built far to the east in Texas and, closer, in Sonora
and Arizona. The first reason is that Alta California was a great distance from
the capital and could be reached only by a hazardous route across a rough
and inhospitable land or along a rugged coastline by sea. The second is that
the missions were founded at the time of the decline of the Spanish influence
and consequently lacked not only political but financial support. Only a few
years after the founding of the last important mission, Santa Inés, the first of
the Mexican revolutions broke out, in 1810.*

*After the disastrous secularization laws were passed in the 1830's, many
of the missions rapidly fell into ruin. The story of their despoilment, the
forced sale of the lands, the attendant scattering and impoverishment of the
once protected Indians, is one of the truly black chapters in the history of
California. Under these circumstances many if not most of the mission buildings fell into ruin. Some remained partially inhabited, and one only—Santa
Barbara—never completely lost its status as a Franciscan church. Several of
the mission churches have completely disappeared—not even a semblance of
a ruin remains. Of others only a few fragments of adobe or brick walls here
and there are left. At Santa Cruz a new and modern church replaces the old.
The San Francisco Solano (Sonoma) chapel has lost all true character of a
mission and, despite restoration, is merely a museum with little of the mission about it but its outward appearance. Nothing remains of San Rafael.
Of San José only a small piece of a quadrangle building still stands. Santa
Clara is represented by a modern church. The one ruined mission that stands
isolated, and which is being gradually restored, is that known as Soledad. No
pictures of the vanished ones—Santa Cruz, San Rafael, Santa Clara, and San
José—are included in this book, although these missions are frequently re-
ferred to in the text.*

*For assistance in gathering source material I am much indebted to Fathers
Thaddeus Kreye, O.F.M., and Maynard Geiger, O.F.M., of the Old Mission
in Santa Barbara. Edith Buckland Webb, author of the definitive work* Indian Life at the Old Missions, *has contributed from her vast store of information. The pastors at all the extant mission churches have also encouraged the
work and given much help. There are few books on mission architecture beyond those that merely describe. Newcomb's book,* The Old Mission
Churches of California *(1922), is a standard reference work, but more recent
studies and explorations have proved it to be inaccurate in some areas. George
Kubler's* The Religious Architecture of New Mexico *is an excellent and scholarly study of construction methods which in many instances had parallels in*

California. Father Zephyrin Engelhardt's series on individual missions is in-valuable to the student of early California history. I am also especially grate-ful to June Main and Elaine Gillson for their painstaking work on the man-uscript, and to Beth H. and George P. for patiently looking over the material as it developed. I am indebted to James McMennamin for his assistance with the explanatory drawings, and to Rolf Linn for his work in copy reading. And, lastly but of first importance, I am indebted to Hugo Rudinger for his bromoil photographs. These have captured what can be considered much of the orig-inal simplicity and beauty of the missions and show them, without any of the crassness of the twentieth century, as they might have looked more than a hundred years ago. The photographs were made especially for this work and were printed by a painstaking and beautiful process.

KURT BAER

Santa Barbara, February, 1957

Contents

IV

V

Illustrations

I

Introduction

The colonizing and Christianizing of the Californias was long in being brought about. Early in the seventeenth century, Sebastian Vizcaíno had explored the coastline of California. Before him, as early as 1542, Rodríguez Cabrillo had sailed along the coast. But it was not until more than a century later that the occupation of California was finally undertaken. The arid, rugged, and thinly populated peninsula of Baja California had been colonized by the Jesuit Order under the zealous guidance of Father Juan María Salvatierra. In October, 1697, with six other men he had established the first mission, Nuestra Señora de Loreto, near the southern tip of the peninsula. For the next seventy years the Jesuits colonized that land, converting the natives, teaching them crafts, agriculture, and animal husbandry, and erecting a chain of fourteen missions extending northward almost to the head of the Gulf of California. By 1735 the system was firmly established. The proselyting of the Jesuits came to an abrupt end in 1767 when their order was expelled from Mexico.

In 1768 the Franciscans, who for more than two centuries had had great success in New Spain, replaced the Jesuits as the directors of the California mission system. The Dominicans petitioned for a share in the spiritual conquest of the north, and the Franciscans, through arrangement with the government, surrendered control of the Baja California missions to the Dominican Order. The Spanish Crown in 1770 ordered the division of the province into Alta (Upper) and Baja (Lower) California. Until the end of the colonial period the Franciscan Order was virtually in sole religious control of Alta California.

A new era of colonization began auspiciously with the appointment of José de Gálvez as *visitador-general* and Captain Gaspar de Portolá as governor of Baja California. The appointment of Father Junípero Serra from the Franciscan College of San Fernando in Mexico City as *presidente* of the "California missions" completed a remarkable and history-making triumvirate that was to have profound influence on later history. These three men were backed by one of the greatest of Mexican viceroys, the Marqués de Croix. In

Alta California, as in New Mexico, missionary and colonial history were closely interwoven.

Soon after the occupation of Baja California by the Franciscans, who set about restoring order in the missions, plans for new missions were made. In the brief interval between the departure of the Jesuits and the coming of the Franciscans, the occupying soldiery had all but undone the years of patient Jesuit work. Proposals were made by Gálvez for the occupation of Alta California, which included that vast and then unknown area that is now the state of California. Rumors of Russian penetration southward from Alaska primed the effort.

The founding and establishment of missions depended on factors which eventually made them great centers of farming and industry. The first requisite was a numerous Indian population that provided material for conversion, the principal aim of Serra. Second, the site should have available fresh water and good arable land for crops and grazing. Third, but of less importance, was the proximity of the site to the ocean; if possible, it should be near a bay so that shipments of goods could be made and received.

Two padres (*frailes*) were invariably assigned to a mission. Although the work was evenly divided, one padre as a rule had the charge of spiritual, the other, temporal matters. Both men instructed the Indians and, later with the assistance of imported craftsmen and the occasional though undependable help of the military, taught them crafts and agriculture. Of prime importance was the teaching of Christian doctrine and the various prayers and responses of the liturgy, at first in the native tongue and, as the neophyte (the Christianized Indian) improved, in Spanish. In many missions music was emphasized, and eventually good choirs and even orchestras were trained. The first crafts taught the Indians were carpentry and "brickwork"; then other crafts such as wood carving, weaving, pottery making, and working in leather and in iron. Labor outside the shops consisted of various kinds of agricultural work, stock raising, and the attendant butchering and tanning. The padres believed that busy hands were less liable to wrongdoing.

By January, 1769, the Alta California project was under way. Three missions were to be established: one at San Diego, one far to the north at Monterey, and one (to be called San Buenaventura) about half way between the two, on the channel. The expeditions used the old maps prepared by Vizcaíno a hundred and fifty years earlier. The land and sea expeditions left La Paz at almost the same time. Father Serra rode with Portolá, who led one of the two land expeditions. By July 1 all had arrived at the harbor of San Diego, and on July 16 Serra founded the first of the Alta California missions, dedicating it to San Diego de Alcalá in honor of whom Vizcaíno had named the bay. Two days before the founding, Portolá, with a small company of men, had left for the north on what is perhaps the most historic land trek in the annals of

California. Searching for Monterey Bay, shown on Vizcaíno's map, he passed by it without recognizing it and marched on until he was stopped by the Golden Gate. On his return to San Diego he found the small group almost decimated from starvation, illness, and Indian attacks. However, on March 23, 1770, the tide turned, for the relief vessel *San Antonio* sailed into the harbor. The colonization of California was saved.

Portolá soon set out on another expedition in search of Monterey Bay. With Lieutenant Pedro Fages and Father Crespi, who kept a diary of the expedition, he walked the nearly six-hundred-mile distance, while Father Serra went by ship. On June 3, 1770, Mission San Carlos Borromeo was founded on a site now within the town of Monterey. The next year a more desirable site in the valley of the Carmel River was selected, and in 1793 the present building, commonly called Carmel Mission was begun. By the summer of 1823, nineteen more missions had been founded. Serra, one of the great missionaries in the New World, founded nine missions before his death in August, 1784.

The second presidente of the missions was Father Fermín Francisco de Lasuén—in almost every way as great a missionary as Serra. He was presidente for eighteen years and during that time established nine missions. Father Estevan Tapis was the next presidente. Santa Inés was the only mission established during his term of office; it was also the last of the southern missions. At a much later date two missions north of San Francisco were built: in 1817 San Rafael Arcángel was founded at San Rafael as an *asistencia* of Mission San Francisco (Dolores); and in 1823 Mission San Francisco Solano was founded at Sonoma. The mission period was approaching its end.

From their very beginnings the California missions experienced many hardships. Although the coastal Indians were on the whole far less troublesome and were more readily converted to Christianity than the Indians of other areas, they nevertheless were difficult. They had little in the way of an established culture. Having progressed only slightly beyond the most primitive stone age, they had few arts, no pottery, no architecture, and no organized religion. They were on the whole an extremely primitive people who subsisted mainly on shellfish, small animals, and seeds, roots, and acorns. But once having come into the Franciscan fold, they learned rapidly. They became trusted charges and, with few exceptions, exemplary members of a new community. The mission system was a complex one, in its essential form dating from the period of the Spanish conquest in the early 1500's. The Spanish kings and the subsequent regional or territorial governments placed the religious brotherhoods in charge of the missions, sometimes giving them control not only of spiritual but also of economic matters. The padres in California knew from the outset that eventually the missions would be secularized and the Indians would be "liberated." Theoretically, secularization would be effected after ten years of religious administration. Where the natives were more civilized, and where they could establish themselves as genuine citizens protected by the laws of the state, secularization was a relatively simple matter. But in California the situation was otherwise. Almost from the very beginning unfortunate clashes between the necessary military escort and the padres took place, invariably because of the mistreatment of the Indians by the soldiers. As the missions grew—some of them held in fief for the Indians enormous tracts of land—their prosperity increased. The missions were the only thriving centers of agriculture and cattle raising in an otherwise virgin land. The material success of the diligent Franciscans and their neophyte charges aroused the jealousy of the civil administrators. As a result, from about 1832 until the United States government took possession in 1846, much if not most of the mission lands and virtually all the buildings were confiscated illegally.

Originally the missions were financed in part through the Pious Fund, an aggregate of moneys and properties first set up and administered by the Jesuits. Donations from individuals and groups formed the basis of the fund, and it was increased through investment and further gifts. When the Jesuits were expelled in 1767, the fund, which had grown to sizable proportions, was confiscated by the government. Moneys however, were still allotted for missionary work. It must be remembered that the conquest of new territories by the Spaniards was always twofold—religious and economic or territorial. The sum of $1,000—in those days 10,000 pesos—was allotted for each new mission, and that sum had to provide for everything, including the transportation of materials. Since the amount provided was seldom enough, the newer missions depended on the older and established missions for material support in the form of livestock, seeds, plants, clothing, and church goods. The padres themselves were allowed a small annual subsistence fund. The missions actually cost the government very little, although the Crown did equip the guards and provide for their keep and made occasional gifts of various kinds. Very gradually at first, and then with increasing rapidity, the garrisons and in some places the entire presidios came to depend on the missions for support. Not only did the missions provide food, but sometimes clothing and even labor—all on account. Needless to say, neither the missionaries nor the Indians were ever repaid.

As the first missions prospered, new ones were planned. It was never just a simple matter of planting the Cross and inducing the pagans to learn the way of Christianity. The founding of a mission required the consent of virtually the entire bureaucratic organization of the viceroyalty, as well as the Church hierarchy in Mexico; the approbation and permission of the Franciscan or other religious college was needed; and lastly, but of vast importance for the success of the undertaking, the coöperation of the provincial governor. Without the governor's permission not much could be done, in spite of viceregal authorization and support. But little could stand in the way of so zealous and inspired a missionary as Serra, though collisions of temperament between him and the prosaic and often shortsighted men in charge of temporal matters were inevitable. It was not uncommon for supplies to be delayed, or for permissions to be withheld. But eventually the missionaries won out.

The initial setback to the mission system came soon after the Hidalgo revolt in Mexico in 1810—the first of the series of revolts that resulted in the establishment of Mexico as a nation independent of the mother country. Financial support from the Pious Fund, on which the missions depended, ceased for a time; stipends were sent only intermittently in the next few years. Finally, in 1832 the entire Pious Fund was appropriated by the state, and although support of the missions continued sporadically until about 1836, the amounts allotted to them were very small.

The constant political turmoil in the national capital directly affected the missions. From 1831 on, a series of unscrupulous California governors took advantage of the situation and, invoking the ancient rule of secularization, attempted to confiscate the missions, sell the lands for profit, and "free" the Indians. There was much confusion, though an occasional governor was friendly to the Franciscans and understood their plight and that of their charges. Although the Franciscan missionaries knew that the law called for secularization within ten years, they also knew that in so short a time the Indians—and especially the California Indians—would never be ready for it. Under the Franciscans the Indians were better housed, better fed, and better clothed than even before, and though they had to work, there was little reason for them to complain. The Franciscans were fighting a losing battle. The secularization laws were passed in 1833 and 1834. From then on, with almost no interruption, the missions were subject to legalized pillage. A few padres remained in the churches. Most of the buildings were rented or sold, and almost everything of any value was disposed of. The buildings fell into ruin; only a few escaped total destruction—San Buenaventura, San Miguel, Dolores, Santa Barbara, Santa Inés, and San Gabriel. Between 1842 and 1850 much of value in the way of records, church goods, paintings, sculpture—even the very tile on the roofs and floors—disappeared.

Eventually a rather large portion of mission property, particularly the church buildings, was restored to the Church. A few missions have reverted to the Franciscans; several are secular parish churches; three are state monuments; and a few are only memories of the most glorious and romantic period of evangelization in the country. The mission lands were irretrievably dispersed through land grants made by governors during the Mexican upheaval.

With the return of the mission buildings and properties to the Church, the restoration of the buildings has been a continuing process for many years. One of the great problems confronting those who plan and execute a restoration is to decide which architectural phase of the mission building should be restored. It is reasonable to assume that a correct restoration of any given mission is impossible; for structural changes, improvements, enlargements, and what might be termed modernizations were made even by the Franciscans during their occupancy before secularization. In the late 1890's much well-meaning, but totally incorrect and even ruinous, "restoration" took place. Reconstruction for the purpose of making a leaky church and its quarters habitable can scarcely be called restoration. Sometimes the interior was given a thorough cleaning, with generally disastrous results to the original decorations. Wholesale replacement of mission-period altars and furniture by hideous French gothic pieces was the rule. The outside appearance of many of the mission buildings, as at Carmel and San Luis Obispo, was radically changed.

Reconstruction and repair are not the same as restoration. Of necessity there has been continuous repair and not infrequently reconstruction. After the *campanario* at Mission Santa Inés collapsed in 1911, the first reconstruction was inaccurate. In 1947–1948 the campanario was once more rebuilt; the original design was followed, though concrete was used for the core. To have restored the original with adobe and brick would have been to invite future disaster. Necessarily, more substantial materials than adobe were substituted wherever it proved expedient. In 1925 Mission Santa Barbara was shattered by the earthquake, and during its subsequent reconstruction several engineering methods foreign to the original were introduced. Steel and concrete used in the reconstruction did not change the outward appearance of the building. Chemical disintegration of native stone and mortar, however, made necessary a second reconstruction. In 1951–1953 extensive work was done on the subterranean foundations, and a new stone facing was put on the towers. With few exceptions, almost all interior decorations and furnishings were changed in both periods of "reconstruction." The exterior is a good example of restoration; the interior, including the reredos, is a good example of reconstruction and remodeling.

The Santa Barbara restoration can be called a successful one, and within the past several years the restoration problem has been more intelligently approached. Perhaps the outstanding example is the restoration undertaken in the 1930's at Mission La Purísima Concepción. After years of total neglect, vandalism, and despoliation, the mission buildings were not much more than heaps of rubbish. Yet, diligent and patient examination of records and photographs, interviews with early settlers, and archaeological and structural study has made possible the almost complete restoration of the compound as it existed before secularization. Where details of the original were lacking, such as in wood carving, in colors, and in furnishing, extant examples from other missions were copied. Even the adobes and the burned bricks were made in the original manner. The mission compound no longer belongs to the Roman Catholic Church; it is a state park, administered by the Division of Beaches and Parks. Much the same situation obtains at Mission San Francisco Solano in Sonoma, where the second chapel and the adjoining *convento* have been restored.

At San Antonio a careful restoration is in progress, and much of the original character of the buildings is being recaptured. The work is being done by the Franciscan seminarians under expert direction.

The work at Carmel Mission, though deviating here and there for the purposes of expediency, has been generally very good. Some of the details, however, are not authentic. Mission San Luis Rey has similarly been restored and, since it houses a seminary, certain modifications in the disposition of the rooms of one of the "long buildings" have been made. Changes have been made in details of the decoration of the interior walls and the construction of certain physical parts of the church. But the church is substantially as it was in the 1830's. Here, as in several other missions, the pulpit was destroyed and has never been rebuilt.

In the 1930's the restoration of Mission San Diego, possibly the most important mission historically, was undertaken, but the results are not satisfactory. If seen only from the approach on the slope below, the façade with its towering campanario appears rather spectacular; so also does the façade of the "padres' building" extending some distance to the right. Unfortunately this long façade is merely a false front. It is a flagrant example not only of faulty restoration, as reference to any early print or photograph will show, but of incorrect construction. The interior of the church is in no sense a restoration. Granted that San Diego was never the great mission that it might have been, the present appearance of the interior, with its cold, hard, impersonal whitewashed walls, incongruous altar, and the use of modern prints for the Stations of the Cross, is hardly what one would expect. The mission, like so many others, was pillaged and its treasures scattered. It would have been far better had the decorations been omitted and the character of the building recreated through reconstruction.

The almost obliterated pile that remained for nearly a hundred years, Nuestra Señora de la Soledad, is at this writing being restored. The chapel, not the larger mission church, has been rebuilt and refurnished with appropriate pictures and altar decorations. Yet the exterior of the small building lacks the character of the original because of the too accurately engineered corners and roof lines. Where in the original there were subtle deviations of lines from the true vertical or the horizontal, and where wall surfaces were pleasingly uneven, all is now straight, flat, true—and uninteresting.

Thus, supposedly true restoration of many mission buildings is inaccurate in spite of correct dimensions and the simulation of the original appearance. The most important quality of any of the mission period structures was omitted: the handmade character of everything. It was the irregularity of line, the unevenness of wall surfaces, the variegated color and texture, the imperfect right angles that gave to those structures their unparalleled and inherent charm. The modern restorer has invariably chosen to straighten lines, to true corners, to unify the textures; he has ignored the details in his concern for a misinterpreted "faithfulness" to the plans. Any cursory examination of old photographs would reveal the "slightly uneven skyline," the undulating surfaces of both interior and exterior walls. And too often an attempt at "antiquing" is made; false cracks are chipped into new stucco, muddy paint is smeared in places to simulate water drippings.

Unfortunately for historical purposes, true restoration is usually not possible. The tremendous encroachment of modern streets with business and residential properties on former mission lands makes it virtually impossible and certainly impractical even to attempt full restoration. The successful appearance of the mission church depends greatly on the surrounding plot of ground. Those churches in cities—Dolores, San Buenaventura, San Fernando, and San Gabriel—are hopelessly lost. San Miguel, though far from any city, can never be properly restored. A great highway passed almost at the very entrance of the church.

In recent renovations and restorations the problems of modern conveniences (when the building serves as a parish church) must be carefully considered. Lighting is a prime consideration. In the mission period there were only candles and lamps; the effect of glaring electric light bulbs, neon or fluorescent strips, and spotlights is shattering. The same is true of heating devices. To restore a mission architecturally and insert gas or steam radiators may perhaps make for greater comfort, but it is hardly either restoration or improvement. Yet if the churches are used for divine services, as so many of them are, the comfort of the churchgoers must be considered.

When a good many of the missions were given over to the secular clergy in the period 1850–1900, up-to-date altars, plaster statues, and Victorian and art nouveau candelabra and chandeliers were introduced. To many a well-meaning priest the simple, often crude original altar and other ornaments, timeworn as they were, appeared hideous. Gallons of white, blue, green, and brown house paint were generously applied over the decorations made by the neophytes. Old lighting fixtures, carved vigas, even paintings and statues, were disguised; very few were left untouched. This practice was by no means limited to the treatment of the California missions by the secular clergy; most of the pueblo churches of New Mexico and Arizona suffered the same fate. Very slowly, authorities are realizing that these well-intended labors in the late nineteenth and early twentieth centuries did more harm than good. Gradually the anachronisms are being removed. The over-all artistic unity of the mission style should be preserved and the neophyte and colonial heritage made apparent in the correct restoration, even though the feelings of pious but ignorant donors are hurt. In two mission churches a thousand miles apart—the San Miguel church in Santa Fe and the mission church at Santa Inés—the anachronistic decorations have been removed and the original simplicity has been restored.

To keep the architectural heritage of the West from mongrelization, the restoration and preservation of the missions should be in the hands of competent historians, archaeologists, and architects without preconceived ideas of what the buildings should look like. The mere knowledge of the physical dimensions of a building and—since duplication of original materials is not often advisable—the character of the stone, wood, or adobe to be used is not enough; an understanding of the religious and humanitarian motives that prompted the founding of these missions is also needed. The psychology, the tastes, the very spirit of the times must be thoroughly assimilated by those who undertake the restoration of the old missions in order that the result will be a total rather than a partial expression of the original conception.

To achieve this total expression the restorer must go further—he must know the origins of the architectural styles which, though adapted and transformed, are the basis of the structural charm of the missions. There were four such style origins.

II

Architectural Styles of the Missions

The appearance or style of architecture in general, and of any group or single building in particular, is affected by and is the direct result of social and material conditions. The dominant social influence acting upon the missions was religion. The mission compound served as more than a chapel where the Indians could learn and worship. Thus the principal feature of the settlement was the church building; it was the focal center of the unit. As the nature of the Roman Catholic religion influenced the construction of the chapel (since it called for a large enclosed space for group worship), so also did the Indian himself influence the building of the compound. This counterinfluence can be seen in the walled enclosures, the generally unbroken outside walls, the sometimes fortress-like appearance of the church itself. The third social influence, and one of very considerable importance, was economic. Where funds were unlimited, great projects could be unstintingly developed. The reverse was true in California. To make the most of the niggardly funds allotted to them, the padres substituted materials and improvised short cuts to create effects, sometimes imitating the grandiose through the use of paint and plaster and wood.

The influence of materials has always made itself felt in architecture. The country itself, the terrain, the availability of wood, stone, water, and other materials—all these have always profoundly affected style in architecture. And the medium used or adapted in turn affects the method of construction and in general limits the expression of that material. To this must be added the all-important element of labor itself. Nowhere can this interrelationship of materials, methods, and labor be seen to better advantage than in the mission structures of California and New Mexico.

To the social and material influences that resulted in the California mission style must be added a third factor—preconceived style. Every architect must of necessity take into consideration the use or purpose of the building, the materials available, and the methods of construction, and he must fuse these into a logical expression of the fundamental reason for a building—that it is a shelter. But he invariably will conceive of his structure according to an ideal that he has either known or experienced, or which he is creating anew. The mission padres were not artists as such. In spite of this and the fact that they borrowed from past styles, they created an architectural style that has had lasting influence. Theirs was not a matter of engaging a designer to form for them new buildings in a virgin land.

The "architects" of the missions were the padres themselves. Since they were also the contractors and overseers, the teachers as well as laborers, they created and executed almost singlehanded these ambitious building projects. Obviously the Franciscans were self-trained in architectural design and construction. A few had some more formal training, others had practical experience. With a plan in mind, which was often subjected to change, they worked out the problems of building as the problems presented themselves. The mission compound had its reason for being, and in its final form expressed the very nature of its purpose: to serve as a house of worship, a residence, a school, a workshop, and not infrequently, a fortress. The climax of this compound was the church, toward which all the inventiveness and the artistic resources were directed. Only at a few missions did the padres have the benefit of the assistance of trained Spanish and Mexican masons. The construction, and perhaps even some of the planning, of Missions San Gabriel, San Luis Rey, and Santa Barbara, was under the supervision of the master mason, José Antonio Ramírez. Some records credit Ramírez with having been the architect for San Luis Rey and also for the Plaza church in Los Angeles. The results of the padres' labors are both eclectic and indigenous. And although the mission churches follow a pattern to a certain extent, individual differences make each distinctive. The character of the padre was bound to be reflected, somewhat at least, in the building he produced. Father Antonio Peyri designed San Luis Rey; Father Antonio Ripoll, Santa Barbara, Father Antonio Cruzado and José María Zalvidea planned San Gabriel, and Father Muguría, Santa Clara. Two of these are outstanding landmarks.

THE SOURCES OF THE STYLES

The actual decorative or architectural style of each church had its origins in old Spain, where construction on the grand scale was an inheritance from the Romans, and ornate decoration a legacy from the Moors. The architectural style was strongly influenced by climate, geography, and natural resources (stone, timber), and—of great importance to the realization of the goal of the builders—the social and political temper of the time. Certainly had political conditions been more settled and the economy more stable and prosperous, the ultimate appearance of the missions might have been vastly different.

One style in Spanish and Spanish colonial architecture has endured for twenty centuries, as it has elsewhere in southern Europe: the Roman, or classical, style. It is characterized by an almost somber dignity and restraint, especially in the façade architecture of what later was called the neoclassical style of building. In Spain this style was native, for the Romans had occupied that country for several centuries. The columns, smooth or fluted, with simple or complex capitals, the pediments often with high-relief sculp-

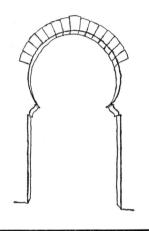

Fig. 1. Types of Moorish Arches: *above*, the typical Moorish horseshoe arch; *below*, the small carved arch on the reredos at Mission San Juan Bautista.

ture, the decorative friezes—all were integrated into later architecture. The first widespread reappearance of this older style occurred in the late fifteenth and the sixteenth centuries. It has been known as the Renaissance style. Its greatest exponent in Spain was Juan de Herrera (1530–1579).

The severe simplicity of the Herreran architecture as evidenced in his Escorial was reflected in a modified manner in the cathedrals of Puebla and Mexico City. This was the "official" style; hence it is seen throughout Latin

America chiefly in the cathedrals rather than in the "Order" churches of the colonial period. Much later, toward the end of the eighteenth century, the neoclassic style made its appearance. In this late phase, a revival of purity and simplicity of proportion and restraint in decoration spread to all architecture, and it profoundly affected the California mission style. Just previous to the establishment of the Renaissance style, the plateresque had been popular in Spain. This was an extremely beautiful style, decorative rather than functional; it was so called because of its dominating ornamental tracery, which resembled somewhat the work of the *plateros,* or silversmiths. It was a combination of Gothic tracery and Moorish all-over pattern, held together by the order and plan of the classical style. Fine examples are to be seen in Salamanca, Spain, and on the façades of late sixteenth-century Mexican churches such as Tepoztlán and Acolman.

The most distinctive contribution to the style origins was made by the Moors in their seven-hundred-year occupation of Spain. Theirs was a luxurious ornament, filled with complex geometrical patterns often of carved stone and alabaster and wood, more commonly of stucco; varicolored tile work; graceful and often intricately conceived arches; bulbous or onion-shaped domes. The adapted Moorish style is known as Mudejar. Its impact was felt in virtually all phases of subsequent Spanish art and architecture. Many of the Moorish buildings, including some of the mosques (as at Cordova), were merely taken over by the Christians as they gradually reconquered Spain and were not rebuilt. Moorish methods of construction and decoration were adopted by the Spanish and were transplanted to the New World. All the characteristics of Mudejar architecture, except the rich tile work, are to be found in one aspect or another, in simplified form, in the missions. It is in the treatment of the heads of arches for doors and windows that the Moorish-Oriental heritage persists most conspicuously in the mission buildings. Common as these rather exotic arches are, one variant is not seen in California. The type of arch that describes more than two-thirds of a circle—the horseshoe arch—was not used here, probably because of problems of construction. This arch was widely used in Spain even in areas unaffected by Moorish contact. It is very doubtful that any specific buildings or parts thereof, either in Spain or in Mexico, served as models for the mission work. Yet, since Serra and other missionaries worked at one time from Querétaro, it is possible that they were directly influenced by some of the numerous and excellent examples of Mudejar architecture in that city.

The Romanesque and the Gothic were rare, if used at all, in mission architecture. The vaulting in the Carmel mission has some resemblance to the Gothic; but the construction is different, for there are no massed piers to carry the thrust of the arches. Nor are there any Gothic arches in the many arcades. Here and there a pointed, or nearly pointed, arch is seen, but as a rule, arches of this type were an expedient of construction rather than an imitation of a particular style.

In countries which had already a developed or perfected indigenous style —as for example, Mexico and Peru—transplanted architecture often took on local characteristics. These might appear in details, or in techniques, such as the manner of finishing the stone; or the local methods of construction might even be adapted to the imported style. No such adaptation was possible in California, for there was nothing to go by—no local architectural heritage or contribution. The California Indians had no architecture. Hence the Franciscan style developed. This was a fusion of earlier forms, adapted to purely local needs and further modified by the availability not only of materials but of workmen. Actually the building forms of sixteenth-century Mexico were repeated in California, as they had been earlier in New Mexico, surviving through adaptation and transformation.

Perhaps the greatest differences between our missions and their Mexican or Spanish prototypes are due to the fact that masons, artisans, workmen, materials, and, most important, moneys for financing elaborate structures were not available to the extent they had been when, more than two centuries earlier, a similar program was undertaken in Mexico. At the very beginning of the building program in 1769, and for a number of years afterward, there were no masons, architects, or engineers. The first mission structures were hardly worthy to be called buildings and were definitely of a temporary nature. They were *enramadas*—brush huts thatched with tules or other materials. Within a short time the first "permanent" structures were built. Even these were of a primitive nature when compared with later buildings on the same or near-by sites. No original mission structures are extant—all have long since disappeared. Most of the second and even later church and quadrangle buildings underwent successive changes. Some of the changes were due to growth: in many places larger churches and more extensive living and working quarters were needed as the number of neophytes increased and the material prosperity of the mission community grew. Other changes were made to repair earthquake damage, for earthquakes were many and often severe. Most of the existing structures were erected after the earthquakes of the winter of 1812, which toppled almost every large building on the Pacific Coast. And still other changes were made when buildings through use had deteriorated to the point of needing repairs. These repairs often involved a good deal of reconstruction, in which structural and often architectural changes were made.

The missions as examples of Spanish colonial architecture must therefore be considered on the basis of the most recent buildings rather than of the original structures. It will be seen, finally, that the style is not Spanish, nor Mexican, nor Moorish, nor Indian, but a distinctly individual one that can best be called California Franciscan. All the mission churches in California

Fig. 2.   Mudejar Arches in the Missions: *above*, Mission Santa Barbara;
below, left, San Buenaventura; right, San Luis Rey.

were not alike in style, however; each had its distinctive character, for the individual padre and the local conditions left their stamp on the building. The California missions were more similar to those of New Mexico than, for example, to those of Florida, Texas, or even Arizona.

THE BUILDING MATERIALS

Among the factors influencing this stylistic difference between the California buildings and their supposed prototypes in Mexico were the materials used in their construction. The padres had been trained and for the most part educated in Mexico; the earlier ones had come from Spain. Most of the large churches, such as San Fernando in Mexico City, Santa Cruz in Querétaro, and the Guadalupe in Zacatecas, whence the majority of the Franciscans were drawn to carry on the apostolic work, were tremendous and most of them were very elaborate buildings. Parts of some of them dated from the sixteenth century. All were superbly constructed, for the Spaniards were everywhere excellent builders and, furthermore, had the services of men who for generations had been good builders. In California, good building materials were not always at hand, nor were there the scores of skilled workmen which elaborate church construction required. Substitutions of materials therefore had to be made. Before 1790 no churches or buildings of complex construction had been erected in California. In that year the padres placed a request, through Governor Pedro Fages, for fifty-one artisans as well as a number of teachers. Without skilled masons no stone churches could be erected, and with the experiences of Mexico behind them, the California missionaries were impatient for trained assistants. On occasion, artisans from the visiting supply boats did help out with carpentry at the missions. But this was common only in the port areas—at Monterey, San Diego, and San Francisco. Even later, when the Indians (who were quick to learn) had become adept at construction, the old methods were used. And methods of construction depended to a large degree on the materials employed.

The astonishing character of the missions and the communities surrounding them in an otherwise virgin land no longer gives cause for wonder. But in the early nineteenth century, the famous world traveler A. Duhaut-Cilly wrote of Santa Barbara:

Here, on the contrary, everything is in the rough, even to the men, and the first care of the builder has been to form his workmen. Out of the mere earth he has had to make bricks and tiles; to cut immense trees, far away, and to bring them, by physical strength, over roads marked out expressly across ravines and precipices; to gather, at great expense, on the seashore, shells to make into lime; finally, everything, to the most trifling, connected with this edifice, has cost preliminary labors, which must have increased the difficulty very much. One is, at the same time, astonished at the boldness of the plan and the perseverance in its execution: only a boundless zeal for the spread of religion can have made Padre Ripoll conquer over so many obstacles . . . (See "Quotations" on p. 69.)

The first structures, as might be expected, were of no architectural consequence; in fact, they could scarcely be called buildings. Shelters they were, but crude ones. "A house of poles . . . divided into two rooms, plastered, and roofed with grass . . ." Such was the "description" of the first mission church at Santa Barbara, recorded in one of the *informes* of 1787. The "plaster" presumably was mud. At this early date probably no lime plaster was manufactured at the mission, though some may have been brought up from Mission San Buenaventura, some thirty miles southeast. Lime was obtained from the vast supply of sea shells, or from limestone, or, occasionally, from fossil beds. At a later date every mission had its lime-burning pit or kiln, for the need for this material was very great, since virtually all wall surfaces both inside and out were whitewashed.

Such "first" buildings were of wood, constructed of pine or other wooden posts set close together and then daubed with clay both inside and out. This rather crude but widely used method of building shelters, huts, and enclosure walls was known as the wattle-daub method. Whenever it was possible this surface was coated with "whitewash"—which suggests that lime kilns were in use and that an enterprise of some importance was well under way at an early date. Very likely these early structures continued in use as the more permanent ones were being erected and, if they did not interfere with important changes, were retained for purposes other than the original ones. As a rule, these structures had roofs of poles over which alternate layers of rushes and clay were laid until a fairly durable covering was made.

In another type of early construction, forked poles were used to support beams, and the walls were of adobes. The forked poles were used in place of pillars for the support of rafters and ridgepoles. This method of building was commonly used in Mexico and later on was widely prevalent in California. It is quite probable that many corridor roofs were supported in this way. The churches using the forked-pole construction were called *iglesias de horconería*.

In the second stage of mission construction—actually the erection of the first permanent buildings—adobes were used for the walls instead of poles and mud, though the roof was made of poles and rushes as in the earlier buildings. Next to wood, adobe was the most widely used building material. Adobe construction was by no means abandoned when the major churches were built; it continued as a structural material throughout the mission period.

Adobe (from a Spanish word derived from the Arabic word *atob*—mud, plaster) is a rather sticky clay, widely found in the coastal ranges and valleys of California. The word is also used for the sun-dried brick made from this clay, as well as for any building constructed of this material. Unfortunately, many writers have noted that "it was built of *adobe* or brick," without making a clear distinction between sun-dried adobe and burned brick. Besides adobes (the sun-dried clay blocks), bricks, tiles, pipes for drainage, and crude pottery were made from the clay. In fact, adobe can be said to have been the principal material used in building, because good stone was almost universally lacking. The adobe "bricks" were of several kinds. The true adobe is made of clay, with an admixture of chaff, straw, at times manure, and sometimes fragments of tile or brick, to give it greater cohesiveness. Most of the local soils had sufficient adhesiveness to make the brick hold together when dried. In the early adobes, chopped weeds and tules were used. Once the proper consistency of earth and water was achieved, the mixture was poured into molds. In general, the brick was about 11 by 23 inches long and from 2 to 5 inches thick. The bricks were allowed to dry in the sun. Even when dry, the bricks were quite heavy, averaging about sixty pounds.

The adobes were laid in courses, "cemented" together with wet clay, and the higher the wall, the thicker it had to be. To prevent buckling outward, massive buttresses were thrown up. Most of the early adobe churches were small. The first adobe church constructed at Santa Barbara in 1789 was 30 varas long and 6 wide (a vara is a little less than a yard). All mission structures of a secondary nature, even the later ones, were as a rule not more than 7 varas wide, this dimension being determined usually by the length of available lumber. Later, much larger churches, such as San Miguel and Santa Inés, were built of adobes, with some stone and masonry used for foundation courses, and burned brick for door and window framing. Yet when the great stone churches were built, from 1813 on, the building procedure was the same as that followed earlier, and many of the walls were very thick and were similarly buttressed.

In spite of their apparent softness and weakness, adobes were often used where there was likely to be considerable stress. Arches in early buildings were often of adobe rather than of post-and-lintel construction, and many adobe arches have survived where they have been protected.

The height of an adobe wall never exceeded thirty-five feet, and when one was that high, the uppermost courses of the adobes were strengthened with timbers set into the wall. Heavy external buttressing that had some counterthrust in the form of what appear to be engaged pilasters on the inside of the building served to prevent collapse of the wall.

Since adobe is an unpredictable building material, methods to protect its surface were devised. If the surface is protected from heavy rains, the structure can last indefinitely; without protection the surface cracks and furrows after a heavy rainy season. Therefore the adobe walls were invariable covered with stucco or lime plaster both inside and out; the less important adobe walls were often merely whitewashed. The plaster was prepared by mixing three or four parts of lime with one of sand, and adding water until the right texture was achieved. During the later period the diluted juice of cactus was added. Cactus "juice" was often mixed with the pigment used in decorating, since it was thought to increase adhesiveness as well as to be more water repellent. Still another method was used to cause the plaster to adhere better to the adobe wall. While the mud mortar of the walls was still moist, bits of broken tile and small stones were pressed into it; the plaster stuck more readily to the varied surface. Quite often the wall surface was scored with shallow furrows, generally (as at La Purísima) in diagonal lines, so that the stucco would adhere better. After the secularization of the missions and abandonment of some of them, these virtually unprotected walls dissolved and collapsed until all that remained were heaps of mud.

At San Luis Rey an interesting construction method was used. Adobe blocks some 18 inches long and 6 by 6 or 8 by 8 inches square were laid in a diagonal pattern. A heavy binding mixture of lime and sand was combined with broken tile, stone, and other fragments to provide a superior bonding for the layer of stucco that covered the wall. Recent examination of one of the side chapel walls reveals five successive layers of plaster over the first "stucco" coating. In several missions a facing of brick laid in sand and lime mortar was placed over or on the adobe wall. The brick surface was then "finished" with stucco or plaster. The system was used at San Luis Rey and San Antonio.

The true bricks (the *ladrillos*), however, were of adobe that was burned or fired (or baked) in a kiln. The size of these depended on the use to which they were to be put; most of them were about two inches thick. The hardness and durability of the brick depends on the heat of the fire in the kiln. Kilned bricks were used where greater strength, durability, and protection from rains was needed. The south wall of Mission Santa Inés is faced in part with ladrillos to insure greater permanence.

The roof tiles (*tejas*) were later developments, replacing the highly flammable tule or straw roofs. Thus, at Santa Barbara, tile was not used for roofing until fully a year after the founding of the mission. The *tejas* were first manufactured at Mission San Antonio, about 1780. After 1790 they replaced the thatch roofs in all except minor buildings. The roof tiles were molded over a section of log which had been split endwise; the ladrillos were made in flat molds, and the clay mixture of these was somewhat stiffer. Both took a rather long time to dry out, after which they were burned or fired in the tile kiln. The ladrillos were made in several sizes, depending on their prospective use. Often they were used as modern common brick is used: for the construction of pillars, door frames, and arches and as molding and facing. In general they were about three inches thick and of various degrees of hardness. Pillars made of these ladrillos (as in part at La Purísima) remained standing long after roofs and adobe walls had collapsed. Bricks for masonry were about 9½ inches square and 3 inches thick; those for the floors were 11 to 15 inches square. The roof tiles were generally about 22 inches long and tapered from 9 to 5 inches in width. The burned brick was used for the lintels, although stone and, more often, wood was used. In the larger buildings the door and window jambs were also of brick. Much depended on local conditions; it is curious that there was no systematic program of engineering. When the bricks were laid in courses to make solid and lasting walls or the strong supports for arches a lime mortar was used.

Brickwork by itself, as in chimneys and balustrades, was often ingenious. Some of the best patterns resulted from the combination of long and short bricks, as in the famous latticed parapet at San Luis Rey.

Floors ordinarily were of tamped earth covered with almost square tiles. In some missions, as at Santa Barbara and Santa Inés, the floor was of *brea*, or bitumen. In others it was of tiles, which were given a harder surface finish, not unlike a crude glaze; in later years these were waxed and polished. In many of the missions the original tile floors—now waxed and waterproofed and re-set in a cement base—are still in use. Walks and passageways were commonly paved with square tiles.

The stone used in the construction of the more important churches was unfortunately not always of the best quality. Ordinarily, a soft sandstone was used—a stone that was common, readily available, and fairly easy to shape. At Carmel Mission, the stone was of a kind that became harder on exposure to air. It was light brown and was fairly abundant. Captain George Vancouver, when he visited Carmel in 1792, commented on its attractiveness and workability. He also noted that at Santa Clara he had been shown "a ponderous black stone, that was intended to be so appropriated as soon as persons capable of working it could be procured." The stone was probably a kind of basalt. This was rarely used in mission construction, probably because of its extreme hardness and heaviness. It was, however, commonly used for grinding stones. Most of the stones used in building San Juan Capistrano were brought from a place near the ocean and were irregular, needing expert cutting. Foundations and some walls often were constructed from unshaped, unsorted field stones taken from stream beds and set in clay or adobe. The average width of a one-story foundation was about three feet. In a few places a volcanic stone was available.

Because of the inexperience of the padres and the difficulty of complex stone construction, there was relatively little vaulting. San Gabriel originally had a vaulted stone roof. This was removed in 1804 because it was unsafe. At Carmel an arched wooden roof was carried on stone transverse arches. The walls of the church were thickened at the top in order to reduce the span, and the thrust was taken up on the outside by heavy stone buttresses. The arch so formed, though similar in appearance to the Gothic, was actually a catenary arch. Of the major churches, San Juan Capistrano had the most stonework, including seven masonry domes. These were wrecked in the earthquake, and all that now remains are sections of the vaulting over the sanctuary. The mortuary chapel at San Luis Rey was constructed partly of stone, as was the baptistery at San Gabriel.

Quite naturally, a true lime mortar was needed to insure a good bond for stone masonry, but on occasion the more primitive mud mortar was used. A practice similar to that found in pre-Columbian structures in Mexico was often employed: small pebbles and stones of various colors were embedded in the bonding mortar. These gave the stone wall a richly varied appearance. In most of the more prosperous missions a combination of brick and stone was used, as at Carmel, Santa Barbara, San Juan Capistrano, San Gabriel, and San Buenaventura. San Juan Capistrano was built almost entirely of stone, including the roof. The interior was of gray sandstone; the walls and the *bóvedas* were of a better quality of yellow sandstone. The work was done under the supervision of a mason and stonecarver, Isidro Aguilar, brought up from Culiacán, Mexico. He died before the building was completed; there must have been another mason to complete the work, although there are no records to that effect.

In buildings of lesser importance a course of stream-bed stones—often of only one layer and without binding—was laid. The adobes were then placed directly on this "foundation" course. In such buildings only the four corners were reinforced, and some mortar was used to bind the stones.

Wood was used as construction material in some places more than in others. In the southern part of the province it was not plentiful. In the north, it was more widely used in secondary buildings, especially after 1825. Often the timbers had to be transported for great distances, for tall timber was rarely found near any mission. Pine was the most common wood; it was preferred because of its usually straight grain, the ease with which it could be cut, and its apparently greater durability. In several missions, roof beams and other supports originally made from poplar and alder, which grew profusely in the canyon areas, were replaced with pine. "Because they were decayed and therefore dangerous . . . all the buildings of the mission [Santa Barbara] have pine wood throughout" states the annual report of December, 1796. The rafters and many of the beams were originally of sycamore and cottonwood. In the San Francisco Bay area, redwood was used. It was more available and more durable than pine. Posts for supporting corridor roofs, as at Sonoma Mission (San Francisco Solano), where they were about six inches square, lasted for many years. Although the existing chapel there was built in 1840, the padres continued to use the older construction methods. In the Monterey district, cypress was available. Oak was not much used, although it is occasionally mentioned in the mission *informes*. Sycamore, found throughout the southern part of the province, was used in some missions.

The beams (vigas) for the ceiling and roof were for the most part evenly spaced. Exceptionally wide spans are rare, and only at the Pala asistencia are there medial supports down the center of the nave. The vigas in most of the California missions are squared (in most of the New Mexican churches they are round) and, at least in the sanctuaries, are decorated with painted designs, as at Santa Inés and San Miguel. Often these beams carried the weight of the roof as well as the ceiling when there was one.

Most of the vigas rest on wooden corbels, which were bonded into the walls and in many instances projected on the outside. The details of the corbels and the manner of carving them will be discussed later.

Still another widely used material was the tule, or bulrush. At first its principal use was for covering the temporary habitations; a thick thatch of these rushes was virtually watertight. At a later date, when tiles replaced the tule, it was still used as a sort of insulation. Interwoven tules, or tules merely laid very close together over the timber framing, were then covered with the nearly semicircular roof tiles. In some buildings the tule roof was covered by a layer of adobes, which in turn had a covering of thatch, providing good insulation against both heat and cold.

The method used in roofing the first churches was almost exactly like that used in New Mexico in pueblo churches of the seventeenth and eighteenth centuries. At first twigs were laid in rows, close together and at right angles to and over the vigas. Sometimes, heavy rushes (as at La Purísima) were used, and again these might be laid at an angle to form a herringbone pattern. This geometrical pattern is possibly an unconscious retention of the Mudejar, or Moorish-Andalusian, heritage of ceiling construction as in sixteenth- and seventeenth-century colonial churches in Mexico, in which boards or planks were used, and which often were richly decorated. Over the layer of rushes, adobe or other earth was packed, several inches thick.

Most of the churches are very narrow. Vaulting as found in Mexico, even in the early churches of the sixteenth century, was not used. In place of vaulting the longest available vigas were employed. As a rule, these beams were at first shaped and squared and later were painted or otherwise decorated. In the small mission churches of New Mexico, the beams (tree trunks) were usually left round; the length and strength of these vigas determined the width of the church. This is an excellent illustration of how the medium to be used determines the methods of construction, and these methods and the purpose of the building influence the style.

It is doubtful that many of the mission-building padres envisioned a completed church according to a preconceived elevation. It is more likely that the ornamental façades were an expression of the builders' ideas and hopes based on remembered buildings but limited by the materials they had to work with. Definite plans and elevations were made for the major churches, and these often were submitted to the authorities in Mexico for review. It is a matter of conjecture whether the persons who passed on the plan and elevations of these provincial churches realized the limitations of the available materials. Certainly they must have surmised that changes and substitutions would be made. It is the substitution of materials that has given to the California missions so distinctive a character.

Perhaps the most remarkable use of substitute materials was in the exterior decoration of the churches. The almost fantastic beauty of the churrigue-resque, the purity of the plateresque, and the severity of the later neoclassic were never completely realized in California. At Mission Santa Clara, for example, the entire façade with its decorative columns, figures of saints, pediments, and other ornaments was painted on the plaster-covered adobe. Red and yellow were the principal colors used. These decorations were on the front of the third church, which was built in 1822–1825; they were executed by the artisan Agustín Dávila with the help of the mission Indians. Such a device can still be seen, but in very modified form, at Mission Santa Inés, where only pillars and a ledge are painted on the façade. In some buildings a very much simplified adaptation of the original models or patterns was made; Mission Santa Barbara, however, has a fairly accurate adaptation of a temple front drawn by the first-century Roman architect Vitruvius Pollio. The difference between Santa Barbara and Santa Clara is obvious. In the former, the façade decoration is architectural; in the latter it is a painted imitation of an architectural and sculptural treatment. Furthermore, all the decoration at Mission Santa Clara was probably pure invention, except perhaps the figures of St. Clare, St. Francis, and St. Anthony, which possibly were copied from paintings or statues belonging to the mission.

A similar substitution of materials can be seen in the interior decoration of the churches, chapels, and sometimes the *salas*. At San Miguel, at Santa Inés —in fact, at almost every mission—the imitation of marble in the interior is very conspicuous. Interiors painted in this way are certainly and literally the most colorful in the mission churches: many of the painted dadoes and the pilasters are garish. Much of this painting has been called Indian work. Undoubtedly the Indians did the brushwork, but the designs are not Indian. Where the Spanish and Mexican churches actually may have had porphyry or marble or tile, painting had to serve in the California churches. Stencils cut from hides were commonly used where repeated patterns called for uniform-ity; the simulated sculptural, geometric and floral borders along the tops of walls and sometimes at dado height were painted with stencils to imitate the classical originals.

In Mexican churches the gorgeous reredos and altarpieces were very large and usually were a combination of stone and wood carving, polychromed sculpture, and painting. In California the decorations on the reredos and altarpieces were only imitations, but they often were very ingenious. A few of the missions possessed reredos that, in spirit at least, had the quality of magnificence: Dolores, San Luis Rey, and probably the destroyed San Juan Capistrano. The elaborate reredos at Mission Dolores and that at Santa Clara, since destroyed, must have been brought up from Mexico. The Dolores reredos is actually the only complete and rather authentic example of this style that dates from the mission period. The one at San Luis Rey is of wood, and parts of it are painted to resemble marble. It is definitely neoclassical in style. In most of the other churches painting was substituted for sculpture. Santa Barbara had a reredos that stood unchanged until the earthquake of 1925. It was a combination of wood sculpture and painting. On several large pieces of canvas affixed to the wall behind the main altar a series of niches was painted in oils. In these niches were painted "statues" of St. Joachim and St. Anne and, above them, garlands and reclining angels. The center of this reredos had a projecting shelf, or bracket, on which stood the almost life-sized wood figure, richly polychromed, of the patron saint. The whole reredos was a flat canvas painting. An almost similar device was used at San Miguel. Fortunately it has scarcely been touched. Here free-standing wooden columns support a rather fantastic architrave above which is a cutout of wood representing the all-seeing eye of God. At each end of the architrave is a huge classical urn, also cut out of a sheet or sheets of very thin wood and cleverly painted. The rest of the ornament is painted. The walls of the sanctuary and nave are decorated in imitation of tapestry-hung bays and projecting cornices and friezes and, in the vicinity of the choir, with an imitation of balustrades. It is an ingenious and exceedingly colorful attempt to give vitality and sumptuousness to an extremely simple, long, narrow basilica-like interior.

At Santa Inés, however, there is no combination; here paint and use of perspective were made to substitute completely for the "real thing." Even a false door, correct in its perspective, is painted on the reredos wall. In the upper tier of panels, centered, a niche has been cut into the wall, to hold the figure of the patron saint. All the rest is illusion—panels, borders, "marble" —to create the impression of grandeur. It is probable that the paintings now in the museum rooms originally hung on the panels; without them the decorations on the painted wall stand out in considerable relief. These works must have been carefully planned. Their coloring is now rather faded. In the original dim light of candles and lamps they must have been far more effective than under the present glare of electric lights.

Another and quite remarkable work of this type now stands on the north wall of Mission Dolores. That this was probably imported rather than made by Indian neophytes is evident in the excellence of the perspective and the drawing of the figures. It is a large, rather allegorical painting approximately twenty-two feet square that at one time was hung or placed before the reredos during Lent. It is on canvas, and consists of sixteen sections, with scenes from both the Old and New Testaments. Represented above is the Last Supper, with Christ in the center, Gideon and Joshua on either side, and the Twelve Apostles. On the next tier below are painted the figures of Faith, Hope, and Charity, balancing and enclosing the tabernacle, which is itself enclosed in a strongly classical frame. At the very foot of the work are two priests with the Wine and Bread offering, respectively, in the lower corners. It is a spectacular work, with the figures in a vast setting of the classical Renaissance type—a representation of an architectural niche complete with an arch, balcony, pedestals for figures, cornices, and capitals. It is, on the whole, excellently painted; unfortunately the artist is not known. The names of three men who either directed or assisted in the decoration of mission churches, however, are known. Thomas Doak painted the reredos at San Juan Bautista, prob-

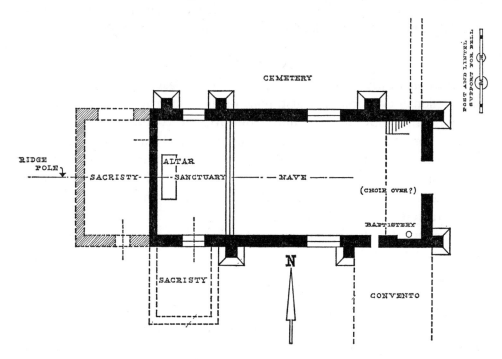

Fig. 3. Generalized Plan of a Mission Church of the Primitive Type.

ably in 1817. Estevan Munras did the elaborate work at Mission San Miguel. And Agustín Dávila painted the façade of the third church of Santa Clara, as well as its interior decoration. Conceivably, the decorative plan was the idea of the padres at each mission, and the intent was always the imitation of elaborate architectural settings.

Although the interior decorations just described are the most conspicuous and striking examples of substitution, there are many others of minor character. In all early descriptions of church construction one remarkable substitution is mentioned: rawhide thongs were used in place of nails and spikes to fasten together the vigas and other beams, especially in the roofing of the churches. The rawhide, tightly wound and tied, shrank on drying and made a rigid joint. Remarkably unaffected by weather, many of the thongs lasted for a very long time. Good nails, long and strong, were commonly in short supply throughout the province, although nails up to fourteen inches in length were made by hand in most blacksmith shops. The iron for this work was at first obtained from Mexico and later, through trade, from Russian and other vessels. When Mission La Purísima Concepción was reconstructed, rawhide thongs were used. The use of thongs for fastening beams not only gives the building an attractive appearance but is an exceptionally effective and practical method of construction.

Rawhide also served as a substitute for glass for windowpanes. The skin was scraped very thin and was made translucent by numerous applications of oil. There is one such rawhide "window" at Mission San Miguel.

THE ARCHITECTURAL TYPES

Primitive and early types.—Because of the continual reconstruction of mission buildings even from the first, none of the extant buildings resemble the earliest forms. Obviously the most primitive, the common wattle-and-daub shelters for both services and living quarters, were abandoned as soon as the first "permanent" buildings were completed. The basic plan of these early first churches can be seen in some of the existing buildings. The details, the size, and even the use of more permanent materials differ from those of the first structures, but the essential character remains. In some buildings, possibly because a particular mission did not become one of the major centers, the more elaborate later style was never used.

The walls of most of the mission churches of the primitive type were made of adobes, wood, brick, and tile. The plan of the church was very simple: a long, rather narrow rectangle, fairly high walls, a single-ridgepole or gable roof. One end was walled off for the sacristy. Over the entrance, in churches of the later forms, was the choir. Walls were constructed of adobes set on a stone and mortar foundation; the walls receiving the heaviest impact of driving rains often were faced with brick. In some churches a sacristy was built to one side rather in the form of an addition or a lean-to (San Miguel). Often it was a continuation of the building to the rear (San Gabriel). The roof was supported by a framework of timbers and covered with rushes and tile. Timber was also used for door framing; brick was sometimes used. The extant mission chapel of San Francisco Solano (Sonoma) is a representative example of the early type. Similar was that of Soledad, now reconstructed. It was, furthermore, a one-story structure that scarcely exceeded the height of the adjoining convento, or, as it is popularly known, the "padres' building." Stylistically it is undistinguished.

There was no bell tower in these primitive missions, nor a campanario; the bells were hung from beams erected usually near the entrance to the church. The mission churches of San Rafael (1817), Soledad, and San José de Guadalupe (1797), were of this type. Of these virtually nothing remains.

Many of these early churches had no ceilings. The Pala asistencia is an example of this type. Beams laid across the top of the side walls span the

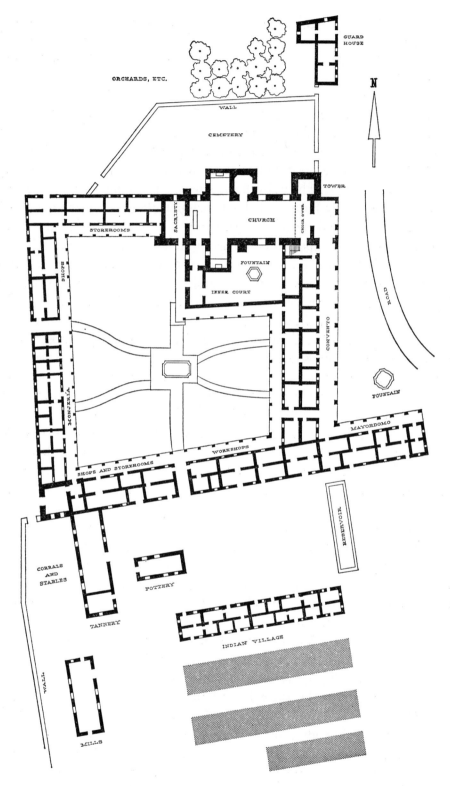

Fig. 4. Schematized Plan of a Mission Community.

width of the nave; the ridgepole is held up by trusses. Upright poles originally supported the crossbeams; these were removed during the "restoration" of 1902–1903. The original sheathing was of willow branches, over which the *tejas* were laid.

This basic style was continued in most of the missions. The larger churches had, in addition, elaborate façades and towers or campanarios; there are several mission churches the style of which is merely a slight elaboration of the basic form. These are, as a rule, of larger proportions and have a few features that give them greater distinction. Mission San Miguel Arcángel is an example of this type. The walls of the nave are much higher than those at Solano and are heavily buttressed. In this church there is a combination of adobe, brick, wood, and tile-roof construction. Except for the reconstructed convento and other compound buildings, it stands much as it did when it was completed more than a hundred years ago. It had no tower, nor campanario; for years the bells were rung from a support erected just to the left of the entrance. The façade of San Miguel is extremely simple. The doorway facing on the present highway has a low arch, above it a small rectangular window gives light to the choir loft inside. The interior is the most poorly lighted of all the missions, for there are only three windows: two near the sanctuary and one over the side entrance on the same wall (the south, or left wall) of the mission. Until about 1890 there was another window on this wall some fifteen feet from the front end. Like the others, it was high up, almost under the eaves. There were no windows on the north side. At one time, to judge from a photograph taken probably about 1910, there was a shallow pediment-like ornament, either in low wood relief or painted on the plaster, over the front entrance. There was no other ornament of any kind.

Projecting from the north side of the San Miguel church and on a line with the sanctuary is a lean-to type of structure that houses the sacristy. There was formerly an addition of a similar type near the front of the church, but this had a gable roof. It has long since been removed. Between these two structures there was at one time an outside door. It is directly across the nave from the side entrance door leading to the convento. At some time this door was in part walled up; and since the wall here is very thick, the resulting niche was used as a confessional. When the wall decorations were later applied, probably between 1818 and 1820, the designs were carried directly across the door, so as to make an unbroken pattern. The wall decorations have already been mentioned. Architecturally there is nothing distinctive about this mission except the row of arches of the convento that faces the present highway. The arches are uneven in width, and as a consequence some have a lower span with a correspondingly shallow curve. The heavy stone campanario at the rear of the church does not date from the mission period; it is a recent and incongruous addition.

Another church still in the basic form is Santa Inés (1804). It is a curious fact that when the church was rebuilt after the 1812 earthquake, adobe was again the predominant construction material, with some brick for facing and for the strengthening of piers and columns. The proportions are similar to those of San Miguel. Here, however, the sacristy is back of the sanctuary (as at Santa Barbara and San Gabriel), and its floor was originally on a somewhat lower level than that of the nave. Except for the adjoining campanario, the church is of primitive form. The walls are very high, with windows high up on both sides. The buttresses are massive and recall to some extent those of smaller outlying Mexican churches. The wall foundations are of masonry, of rather rough stone held together by strong mortar. In several places the walls are more than eight feet thick. The roof originally was supported by wooden, adzed vigas that were decorated. Although these vigas are still in place, they no longer carry the weight of the roof, which is supported by concealed beams.

The façade is similar to that of San Miguel, but there is a definitely classical quality to the decoration. The doorway is a simple Roman arch of brick, with a slight ledge to indicate the simplified capital of the concealed pillars. This arch was painted a dull red, as was the slightly projecting base, which is similarly constructed of brick. The red pigment was probably derived from cinnabar, which had been mined in the neighboring mountains. The arch is fairly wide though not ungraceful. Above it is another, narrower arch within which is a wood-framed window. This gives light to the choir inside. Over the top of the door arch is a slight arched recess in which there is a stone cross in relief. The most striking feature of the façade, however, is the simulated "pilasters" at the sides of the façade. These, like the arch, are painted red; their "bases" and "capitals" have projecting ledges of brick. It was probably the intention of the designer to give the impression of a classical façade. A slightly projecting ledge, at the very top of the wall, extends across the front of the building; it was also painted red. The pediment may have once been decorated, not with sculpture as at Santa Barbara, but with painted devices such as were on the façade of old Santa Clara church. Unfortunately there is no reference whatever to plans or drawings in the extant mission records.

Far more distinctive is the adjoining campanario. The present structure is actually the third. The first collapsed in 1911 during a heavy rainstorm, for like the church itself, it had been built of adobes. The first restoration was inaccurate; in 1947–1948 the campanario was rebuilt of concrete, and the original plan and design were re-created. The design will be discussed later.

The church walls at Santa Inés are of the customary thickness, averaging five feet. In addition to the front entrance, there is a small doorway through a very thick, almost eleven-foot wall, leading into the convento rooms on the left. Access to the choir loft is by means of a stairway inside the church. In the first building—of which this is in part an enlargement—access was from the outside. Opposite this door on the other (north) wall is a deep recess of door height; this, according to some writers, led into a funerary or mortuary chapel—a rather unusual feature in a relatively small church. Only San Juan Capistrano, San Gabriel, Carmel, and San Luis Rey had such chapels. It was probably for an altar of repose. Near the sanctuary are two more doors: the one on the left leads into the patio of the mission, the other into the cemetery on the north side of the church. Some time about 1900 the doorway leading to the cemetery was blocked up, but not completely, only the outer edge being closed. The resulting niche provides a place for a side altar.

Because of the rather charming decorative treatment of the façade, Santa Inés comes near to being a church in the neoclassic tradition. It is indeed strange that more decoration was not carried out on the exterior. Certainly, in view of the fact that an elaborate façade was being constructed not far away at Mission Santa Barbara, such primitive construction and archaic decoration is unexplainable. Finances were probably a determining factor.

Without doubt all the missions at first had such simple façades. The development of the mission façade, from a mere building front to more elaborate structures kept pace with the progressive enlargement of the church building. Santa Barbara, for instance, had four distinct façades, each one more elaborate and larger than the preceding one. In contrast, the conventos usually retained their characteristic one- or two-story appearance regardless of the number of times they were rebuilt or enlarged.

The fortress type.—A second, and historically more progressive style of mission architecture is comparable to what was known as the "fortress style" in sixteenth-century Mexico. Although no California missions are of exactly this type—characterized by heavy buttresses, crenelated walls, and, as a rule, small bell towers—some of them have a few of these characteristics. The most striking example of a mission church resembling a fortress is that of San Gabriel. The very massive walls of stone, the ten thick-set buttresses between the high-placed windows, the severely simple façade—all make it appear very much like a fortress church. The pyramidally capped buttresses that now face the street side of the church were formerly within the quadrangle; these suggest a resemblance to the famous cathedral in Cordova, Spain, which was a converted mosque. It is highly unlikely that the builder of San Gabriel, Father Cruzado, was influenced by this prototype. It is more likely that he took as his pattern the buttressing on such similarly austere churches in Mexico as Huejotzingo, Acolman, and San Francisco Cholula, some of which had very spare decoration along the tops of the walls. It is curious, however, that the buttresses at San Gabriel appear to be the only capped and decorated ones in the California missions. They strongly resemble the crenelation (the *almenas*) of the older Mexican churches.

The present church was begun probably in 1794, but it was not completed until 1806. The church proper is about 142 feet long and 27 feet wide. The construction was similar to that of the churches of Central America: the lower part of the walls up to the height of the windows was of quarried stone. Above that the walls were of brick, probably to lighten the load and lessen the danger from earthquakes. The walls were covered with stucco. The roofing, like that of early Mexican churches, was originally vaulted by means of rather shallow transverse arches, which rested on the pilasters. Unfortunately, and in spite of the strong buttressing, this kind of vaulted ceiling-roof was not strong enough to withstand earthquake shocks. In 1808 this roof was damaged so severely that it had to be removed, and the conventional flat roof of timber and tile was substituted. Nevertheless, the fortress-like character of the building remained. The vaulting in the sacristy was better constructed and remains today; being of greater height and much smaller span than that of the main part of the church, it has withstood all later earthquakes.

Originally the mission had a campanario with a square room on the ground floor, immediately to the right of the entrance, at the northeast corner. It was destroyed in the earthquake of 1812. All that remains is a section of the base that now serves in part as a buttress. There is no description of this tower in any of the records. It is strange that it has never been restored; but this very lack of a tower emphasizes all the more the military character of the building. The present belfry is probably a copy of the upper part of the original one.

Although all the missions had heavy buttressing, few of them actually had a "fortress" appearance. At least, few of them have that appearance now. From the rear, the massive abutments of Mission Santa Inés, of Carmel, and of Santa Barbara have somewhat this character. Usually this is visible on the north side of the church, where the adjoining cemetery was. The inner or enclosure side all too often had minor structures built on to it, some perhaps even covering this whole side. Trees, shrubs, and vines also obscured the walls. The windows, however, in the California missions are generally much larger in proportion than in Mexican churches of this type. In almost all the California missions the windows are very high in the walls.

The plateresque and the baroque.—Although most of the existing mission churches were built during the renaissance of the neoclassic style in the early part of the nineteenth century, several have marked characteristics of the popular earlier baroque style. This is an understandable characteristic of colonial architecture, which, while progressive in one sense, was curiously conservative, especially in Mexico. In that country there were numerous local variations of older styles, all too frequently combined with the prevailing mode. One of these, the plateresque, was a decorative rather than a structural style. It combined the severity and order of the Roman with the tracery and intricate surface pattern of Gothic and Moorish forms. Though short-lived in Spain, where it originated in the fifteenth century, the style found expression in a large number of early colonial churches, particularly in the sixteenth and seventeenth centuries. The most beautiful example of the style in Spain is on the buildings of the University of Salamanca. Early examples of it in Mexico are the façade of the church of San Agustín at Acolman, and those of the churches at Tepoztlán (Dominican), Yuriapundaro, and Actopán. In the plateresque style, most of the ornaments—tracery, medallions, figures, and often animal and bird forms—lie quite flat and are carved in low relief. These designs and patterns are contained within a framework of combined classic pediments, Moorish arches, and various columns or engaged pilasters. Although modified to a large degree in the California missions because of the lack of sculptural detail, the style does nevertheless appear in the façade of a few of them. From the appearance of several façades, such as those of San Luis Rey and the Capilla Real in Monterey, and from that of the side door of San Buenaventura, it would seem that a plateresque decoration might have been achieved had there been the craftsmen to execute the designs. The decoration of the side entrance of Mission San Buenaventura might be clasified as a simplified plateresque. Similar, though it is dominantly neoclassical, is the façade of Mission San Luis Rey. Neither of them, however, has the all-over tracery of delicate motifs characteristic of the plateresque. The very date of these missions, which were constructed in the early years of the nineteenth century, would preclude the use of so outdated a style, and the padres probably had the most up-to-date styles in mind.

Baroque elements are fairly common in the California missions. But the most conspicuous features of colonial baroque—tiled domes, twisted columns, irregular or curving building fronts, and much decorative sculpture—are for the most part lacking. One important and dominating feature is the tiled dome; its absence from the California missions is obviously due to lack of the proper tiles (azulejos) in the province and lack of funds to procure them from Mexico. The other is the twisted, often relief-carved Solomonic column. Examples of both can be found in each of the three important Franciscan churches in Mexico from which the missionaries came: San Fernando in Mexico City, Santa Cruz in Querétaro, and Guadalupe near Zacatecas. Each has polychromed tile domes of considerable splendor, and there are twisted baroque columns both outside and inside the churches. But other features of baroque are in evidence in the missions. These are the curved and reverse-curved pediment forms, as at the Capilla Real in Monterey and the espadaña and campanario at San Diego, and the arched framing over the star window and the unclassical (rather Moorish) dome on the left tower at Carmel. The top of the campanario at San Antonio, though much simplified, has the quality of baroque without its exuberance. The espadaña at San Luis Rey with its nearly floating reverse curves is also of that style. Very nearly all the espadañas and campanarios in the missions are derived from the baroque. It is this suggestion, this implication of a remembered sumptuous style, that has given to these buildings their distinctive character. That there are baroque features in the California churches cannot be denied; but they cannot be compared with those of almost fantastic complexity which decorate both interiors and exteriors of churches in Spain and Mexico. It would be incorrect to classify as pure baroque any one of the missions. Yet one cannot help but feel that had funds and artisans been available California might have had a fine baroque church in true Spanish colonial style.

Almost no baroque elements are to be found in the interiors of the churches, except of course, in the sculptures and paintings. At Mission Dolores there are strong baroque—or rather, churrigueresque—elements in the reredos. The spatial organization and the columns or pilasters are essentially classical. But this reredos, because it does not have flat "temple front" appearance but displays a textural richness in the details of its ornament, is more baroque than classical. It must be remembered that the baroque had so many variations and so many interpretations that there is scarcely one style. This was especially true of colonial baroque; it usually varied as the *ensamblador,* or planner, willed it. Consequently, in the colonial churches the classical style is almost smothered under decorative ornament; Moorish, Gothic, Renaissance, and local motifs are strongly interwoven. Nowhere was this more conspicuous than in the Andean churches of western South America. Thus in many mission churches (Carmel, San Luis Rey, Santa Barbara), arches of Moorish style are interpolated in the otherwise strictly classical architecture: a typical exercise of the baroque. The baroque allowed great freedom of invention, and in the middle years of the eighteenth century broke away from all restraint in the extravagance of the churrigueresque style. However, there is no churrigueresque ornamentation in any mission, except that in modified form on the reredos of Mission Dolores.

The façade of Mission San Antonio has an unusual architectural feature— a sort of narthex with a stepped pediment—which is a simplification of the baroque espadaña. Indeed, it is the espadaña and the campanario that reveal most strongly the watered-down baroque in California. A more comprehensive discussion of these two architectural features will be presented in another section.

Neoclassic forms.—The rise of the neoclassic style in Mexican architecture was a logical reaction against the limitless ornament of the churrigueresque. Led by the architects Tolsa and Tresguerras in Mexico, the movement got under way toward the end of the eighteenth century and became the dominant style of the entire California mission period. All but the earliest of the permanent mission churches were basically classical in their decoration, even those described in this work under other headings. It mattered little whether the building was of adobe (as at Santa Inés) or of stone (Santa Barbara). The classic style reverted essentially to the Roman-temple form, with its triangular pediment, ornamental architrave, niches or pedestals for sculpture, and columns supporting these elements. Prototypes and models of neoclassic churches in Mexico are extremely numerous. The famous churches of north central Mexico, not to mention the cathedrals, had great influence on mission architecture. The Franciscan missionaries in California must have been familiar with the church of Our Lady of Carmen at Celaya and the interior of the Guadalupe church at Zacatecas.

When the first bishop of California, Francisco García Diego y Moreno, was resident at Santa Barbara, he made plans for a "cathedral," for which a design of the principal altar in honor of Our Lady of Refuge was made. It is almost strictly neoclassic. The altar was never constructed. The Bishop's tomb on the Epistle side of the sanctuary at Mission Santa Barbara is completely neoclassic in style. It represents a façade with pediment, pillars, and all parts of a temple front except a door. It is of wood painted to imitate stone and marble. The designs for this and for the altar that was never built strongly resemble the painted reredos at Santa Inés.

Another feature of Roman origin is the raised platform. The Roman temple was built on such a platform. Santa Barbara, the purest example of the neoclassic, San Luis Rey, Dolores, and San Luis Obispo have—or had—platforms approached by steps. Naturally, the contour of the land had an important influence on the treatment of the approach.

Whether plans and drawings and elevations for the mission churches were determined by consulting source books (such as Vitruvius, for Santa Barbara) or whether they were merely designed by a padre-builder or by a paid "architect" is at this point unimportant. The three "artists" who decorated the interiors and the two master masons have already been mentioned. It is interesting to note that the design and plan of almost every painted façade, retable, and reredos were almost completely neoclassic. Naturally, in virtually all mission façades this style was necessarily simplified.

The most elaborate of the church façades, that of the Capilla Real at Monterey, with its suggestion of plateresque, was yet a far cry from Mexican originals. This chapel was never a mission church; it was a chapel erected for the governor and the soldiers of the Presidio of Monterey. Much of the refinement of the details can be attributed to the workmanship. The work was very probably executed under the direction of Manuel Estevan Ruíz, who also supervised the building of the San Carlos church. Ruíz came to California in 1791. It is strange that although both churches appear to have been constructed under his supervision and were built about the same time (Carmel was completed in 1797), they were very different in appearance. Fathers Serra and Crespi very probably planned the Carmel church. Possibly the fact that the Monterey church was important politically (Monterey was the provincial capital of the governors and officials) had some bearing on the style selected for it—the classical style which had been used earlier in Mexico City, Puebla, and other major centers for the cathedrals. Since this church was a government building, approval of the plan, including the *fachada*, had first to be obtained from Mexico. All that remains of the submitted plan is a drawing of the façade and the bell tower, or, more correctly, the campanario. Criticism by the Mexican authorities was to the effect that the building as originally planned was much too narrow. The espadaña type of campanario was intended to take the place of a bell tower; its characteristics will be described later. The chapel was originally constructed with the espadaña; in the "reconstruction" of 1890 this was replaced by the tower.

In the mission church at Carmel there is greater evidence of Indian, hence nonprofessional, work than in the church in Monterey. The baroque designs are described elsewhere. However, the workmanship, if it is that of the neophyte Indians, represents the great technical advances made by them under professional direction within a short span of years. The Carmel church is, for all its simplification, very similar to many village churches in Mexico.

The plan of the façade decoration of the Capilla Real is characteristically bisymmetrical, with a gracefully curving pediment that towers, like an espadaña, over the roof ridge of the nave. The doorway is topped by an arch in simple Roman style and is flanked by rather severe pilasters somewhat derived from the Doric. There is a pair on each side. Between these are niches for statues, the brackets of which are ornate and the arches fluted and scalloped. The pilasters carry a solid entablature of moldings and a bold triglyph-and-metope frieze, topped by an overhanging cornice. Above this are four pedestals, the center two supporting pilasters that frame the low-arched window and extend upward to the second cornice. The two outer pedestals support obelisk-like decorative finials. Above the window there is a triangular pediment. The upper cornice in turn supports a niche with framing pilasters, and the rectangular framing of the niches is topped by the rather flat arch that is characteristic of Renaissance architecture. The niche for the carved relief of the Virgin of Guadalupe is capped by the typical fluted or scalloped shell, here inverted. Very simple, flat pilasters make the framing more severe. There are, however, a few relieving features. At each side of the low arch that caps it, the molding which frames the entire pediment ends in a strong inward-curving volute. A freer volute in low relief decorates the outer edge of the bottom of the pilasters framing the niche. The graceful curve of the outer part of the pediment is repeated in a thin line in relief that begins at the bottom of the pediment and extends outward and downward to the base of the obelisks that top the extension of the outer columns. Decorative finials on the upper cornice and at the right edge of the façade, as well as on the tower, complete the classical ornament. The date of the façade is 1794; it is a good example of the fusion of the baroque with neoclassic.

The most nearly perfect example of the classical style is the façade of Mission Santa Barbara. The building was completed in 1820. The design is almost a direct copy of a temple front pictured in the mission's copy of Vitruvius' book on architecture, the Spanish translation of which undoubtedly served as inspiration for other designs as well. The façade, purely a decorative unit, bears no relation to the towers nor to the arcaded cloister near by. It is strictly bisymmetrical. The large, arched doorway is flanked by three projecting pedestals on each side, none of which bears any sculptural ornament. Where in the Vitruvius plan these and the columns above them were free standing, in the mission they are engaged, projecting only half their thickness from the wall. The shafts are perfectly smooth and end in simple Ionic volutes. These columns support the heavy cornice and the pediment above it. There is no triglyph-and-metope frieze; in its place there is a Greek key or fret design, in fairly high relief, taken directly from the source book. The cornice here, as well as the raking cornice of the pediment, is relieved by a device resembling the Greek guttae. A nonclassical feature of the mission is the stepped espadaña rising high behind the pediment. It is totally unrelated to the design and was merely added to give height to the center of the structure.

Almost as severe, but very different in actual treatment, is the façade of Mission Dolores. This has undergone some changes, especially in the roof line; the present roof appears to act as a protecting canopy. The elevation is in three parts, the lower comprising the rather high base for the thick columns. On each side of the simply arched door are two columns with smooth shafts and very simple capitals. Directly over the door is a bracket that is part of the cornice extending across the front. The upper tier is somewhat pediment-like and is taller than the others. In the center over the doorway is a square window, and above it a slightly larger opening. There are two narrow arched openings between the next pair of columns. Bells once hung in these upper three openings. A balcony railing was at one time in position on the cornice. Originally the six upper columns terminated in small *almena*-like finials. There is no decorative ornament of any kind, nor any tracery to relieve the squat, rather severe character of the façade.

Far more grandiose is the façade of Mission San Luis Rey. The building was probably carefully designed in advance, for there is great unity in all its details. It is rectangular and is flanked by towers: however, only the one on the right is complete. The pediment is roughly triangular and is made up of several sets of S curves; it is decidedly more baroque in outline than it is classical. It is surmounted by a small lantern-like structure having a small niche. This entire structure is actually an espadaña. It is the framing of the entrance door that recalls the plateresque and the classic. There are simple pilasters and moldings ending in finials. Directly above this is a circular window that lights the choir. On each side of the pilasters are deep niches for statues. The interior of the church is more classical than the exterior. The beautiful mortuary chapel will be described later. Its altar, as well as the main altar reredos and those of the transepts are in the best neoclassic tradition. Almost all the details, moldings, and piers both inside and out were made of brick and covered with stucco. The extremely well balanced composition of each area attests to its having been planned in advance by one skilled in such work: Father Peyri and, very likely, the mason José Antonio Ramírez, who also planned and worked on the Los Angeles Plaza church. The Peyri court entrance to the church is as well planned as the façade. Much of the original purity of design, especially in the interior, has been marred by "restoration." In spite of the inaccurate coloring, the interior of San Luis Rey affords the best example of neoclassic mission church style outside Mexico.

The remaining missions in their details offer weak imitations and copies of classical forms. The ruins of San Juan Capistrano imply that the whole was very likely classical in general concept; the remaining engaged pilasters of the sanctuary suggest at least a derivation from that style, although the pilasters are not grooved and the capitals are very much simplified. The dome over the sanctuary was more in the nature of a high *bóveda* than a true dome. All details that must have framed the nine niches of the reredos are gone, but one can assume that they were classical in style.

The little pueblo church Nuestra Señora de los Angeles, better known as the Plaza church, has a very simple and not too well planned façade. It has the arched door, and on each side a slender, half-round, smooth pilaster. Dividing the façade horizontally is a molding, and above it are two rectangular windows. In the pediment, or gable, there is a circular window. Beyond these features there is little to suggest any particular style. Mission San Buenaventura falls into the pattern more successfully, in spite of the fact that its proportions are not so satisfactory as those of Santa Barbara. Unquestionably, the design of the whole front was changed after the façade was completed. The arched door of the entrance is flanked by two pilasters, which are undecorated except for the repetition of the "capital" molding of the "base" of the arch. The outer line of the arch pier extends upward to a cornice which divides the façade and serves as a base for a steep pediment. The molding of this pediment suggests a smaller and earlier gable line. There is a square window in the center, while at the very apex of the gable there is a small corbeled niche. There is no ornamental detail. The recent redecoration has accented the moldings and cornice; a dark-red paint was used. Whether the classical altars or the reredos are the original ones or were made much later is problematical, for virtually the entire interior has been "restored," much of it in the 1890's. Elaborate classical altars were the style at the time of the dedication of this church in 1818, but so much has been altered that it is difficult to determine what remains of the original. During the recent (1957) renovation, the main altar was returned to its original form and lowered to its former level. Unfortunately the renovation and partial restoration did not allow for restoration of the original Indian paintings of urns, flowers, birds, and other forms of decoration that were naïvely intermixed with the rather austere and formal neoclassic forms. In 1808, "the pillars of the baldachin altar in the romanesque style [Roman?] were finished in imitation marble, while the decorations on them were gilded." So reads the entry in the annual report for the mission for that year (now in the mission archives at Santa Barbara). The side entrance, however, is an excellent example of the sculptural decoration that recalls the earlier plateresque style. It has already been described.

At Santa Inés there is token resemblance to classicism. Devoid of any kind of ornament, except for a cross in relief over the doorway, the façade is extremely simple. At the extreme sides of the façade are two red-painted vertical strips that suggest engaged pilasters, and there is a painted cornice that separates the lower section from the "pediment." There is no other ornamentation, except that on the elaborate "classically" painted reredos inside the church. This reredos is certainly the most arresting of its type. It has already been described.

San Luis Obispo has suffered so much from restoration and rebuilding that the only elements of its original style are the "temple front" altar backings in the church. The principal altar reredos has a pair of columns framing the corbeled niche that contains a figure of the patron saint. These support a pediment strikingly similar to the façade of Mission Santa Barbara. There is nothing of architectural interest elsewhere. The details of the façade, combining campanario with espadaña, will be discussed later. Mission Santa Clara's painted façade, long since gone, was in the neoclassic tradition.

Regardless of the details of style, the mission churches and, in many instances, the adjoining buildings had very good proportions, with few exceptions. The wide-spreading, overhanging eaves and the generally low sloping roofs of the California buildings are features which do not appear in the mission churches of Texas, New Mexico, or Arizona. Some of these differences can hardly be due to the climate. The undecorated exterior, which is common to the buildings of the four states, as has been pointed out, had its precedent in the Mohammedan or Moorish styles brought over to the New World. In California, as in New Mexico, the scarcity of workmen certainly limited the amount and complexity of the external decoration. From the strictly artistic or aesthetic point of view, the California missions in general express an over-all sensitivity of line and form, the utmost simplicity of construction, and a freedom from architectural complications. This is all the more remarkable in the face of the crudity of the materials used and the common absence of decoration. As to the general appearance of the individual buildings, the best-balanced design is unquestionably that of the church at Santa Barbara. It is symmetrical, classic, serene. Perhaps the over-all elevation of San Luis Rey has better proportions than that of any other California mission, for its tower is well balanced by the espadaña and the well-integrated convento, on the left, and the espadaña-like entrance to the cemetery, on the right. In this church there is greater architectural and over-all unity between adjacent parts. Carmel Mission is certainly the richest in texture, and it is imposing and has a romantic charm; but the composition is heavy, as in Mission Dolores. The façade of Dolores is so different from any of the others that, like the façade of San Luis Obispo, it stands apart. Though San Gabriel is an imposing mass, it suffers from the loss of the original campanario. Seen from the front, the church is now very plain and heavy. Although each mission has its individual charm, and daring architectural ideas are sometimes expressed in the buildings, the padres, because of their reliance on memory and rule-of-thumb construction, failed to create outstanding works, except for the few mentioned above. The appearance of some of the buildings suggests that the architect lacked a sense of proportion and had no feeling for design; yet the padres produced an architectural style so individual that its influence has been amazing. In the towers, arcades, the simple construction, the spare use of ornament, and the functional plans of the missions, they have made a lasting contribution to architecture.

III

Characteristics of the Missions

The missions, like the mediaeval monasteries, were self-sustaining units, and their organization was similar; yet the differences were substantial. In the California missions, as in the sixteenth-century monasteries of Mexico, there were only a few brothers, or priests. There were only two resident priests in each mission; consequently there was no need for a large number of cells or rooms to house the religious community. The very purpose of the mission called for space for the numerous activities—social, religious, agricultural, and industrial—that took place within its precincts. Hence the mission had to be more than a church with a dwelling place for its padres. Warehouses, storehouses, workshops, and dwellings for the Indians were needed. In some missions these buildings, as at San Juan Capistrano and San Luis Rey, spread over a wide area.

THE MISSION PLAN

Following a pattern set in Mexico in the early years of the Spanish occupation, the mission buildings were arranged round an open square, known as the enclosure. This arrangement is an extremely ancient form for communal buildings. The enclosure as a rule had only one principal entrance, which in ancient times was heavily guarded. The term "mission" is invariably and incorrectly applied to the church building. The mission is not the church alone but the entire settlement making up the quadrangle, including shops, the padres' quarters, and, outside the compound, the Indian village and the quarters for the guards. In early stages of the mission's development the entire area was surrounded by a palisade.

The plan had to take into account the three areas of activity: the religious, residential, and work areas. The church was placed where it would be accessible to all; usually it was at the northeast corner of the quadrangle. There is a curious difference between older Mexican churches and the Californian churches. In Mexico there was invariably a large rectangular walled enclosure in front of the church and the convento. This enclosure, which was called the *atrio*, served various purposes, one of them being protection against trespassers or hostile Indians.

What factors determined the orientation of the church buildings remains unanswered; they do not all face the same way. The majority of Roman Catholic churches in the Americas were built on an east-west axis. Traditionally the sanctuary of the church was at the eastern end of the building. The Franciscans followed this rule throughout their period of construction of churches in the sixteenth century in Mexico. After about 1600, however, there appears to be no uniformity of orientation. In California the majority of churches are on an east-west, or nearly east-west axis, but the sanctuaries are usually at the western end of the building. The exact direction, however, depended usually on the building site and the contour of the land. At very early morning services, a greater amount of light flooded the sanctuary if the doors, facing east, were left open. The problems of interior lighting will be taken up later.

The public area of the mission building faced an open plaza in front of the church. The section of the building adjacent to the church was given over to the private quarters of the padres; this was known as the convento. In addition to the padres' rooms it contained guest quarters, reception *salas*, sometimes a library, and in several missions, a small chapel. In some missions, as at San Juan Capistrano, a long building at right angles to the convento housed the guard and the major-domo and also the guests. It faced the public plaza and was outside the quadrangle. In other missions the guard and the major-domo were separately housed, often a short distance from the main buildings. The Indian village, made up usually of individual houses for the married members of the neophyte community, was a separate unit usually a very short distance from the compound. In general, the Indian village was well arranged as to streets, orientation, and other facilities. Near by were also fountains, *lavanderías*, and cisterns for storage of water.

Behind the convento was the enclosed patio, the remaining two sides of the square being made up of buildings in which the internal life of the mission went on. All the workshops faced this patio, as did the storerooms and the various and sundry activities connected with mission life. Here also were the *monjeria* (the quarters for the unmarried women and small boys), an infirmary, and rooms for the servants. The arrangement within each mission varied, but in each there was sufficient room for weaving, pottery, and other crafts and for the storage of grain, tallow, hides, fruits, and meat and, in one corner, usually the barns for cattle and horses. Sometimes, especially in the larger communities, the padres had a small private patio, an inner quadrangle which the general membership of the mission community did not frequent. It must be remembered that as a rule only two friars or priests lived at and controlled the mission.

In some missions the tannery, the slaughterhouse, the grist mills, and often the pottery and lime kilns were outside the compound proper. Wherever possible there was a wall enclosing even these structures. The various mission activities were usually widespread.

The burial ground (the *campo santo*) was invariably to the north of the church, and as a rule a door from the nave opened into it. In some churches this door is still in use; in several others it has been walled up. The cemetery was enclosed by a high wall and often was divided—one area for members of the community, the other for the Indians. At some missions the Indian burial ground was a short distance away.

In general, the plan of a mission was functional, since the large patio or patios afforded protection, with the surrounding walls, against possibly hostile Indians. For most of the missions such a plan at least was intended although not all of the details were carried out. Where the buildings did not complete the quadrangle, a high wall of adobe capped with tile was built.

The very nature of the Franciscan missionary program, that of Christianizing and making of the Indian a loyal and self-supporting citizen, caused the plan to evolve. Defense and control were important. The most striking example of a mission that did not follow the plan is the second (and now restored) Mission Purísima Concepción; unquestionably, the whole plan was never completed.

The buildings at La Purísima are strung out almost in a straight line along the foot of a sprawling hill. There, the principal gardens, with the fountains, lavanderías, and storage cisterns were in front of the convento proper; the church and its adjacent cemetery were at the far end of the buildings. There was a small enclosed patio next to the workshops.

Many fine examples of enclosures, or patios remain today; not all are open to the public, since several missions—San Luis Rey, San Miguel, and Santa Barbara—are seminaries. Other fine patios—though not complete quadrangles, since not all the buildings that once bordered them have been restored—are at Santa Inés, San Juan Capistrano, and San Juan Bautista. The very large enclosure at San Juan Capistrano is justly famous for the handsome arcades. Excavations reveal the foundations of a large complex of buildings. What is now the tree-filled entrance garden was at one time the plaza in front of the convento. Architecturally the less important buildings were undistinguished, although most of them had colonnades. In general, they were of one story and lacked the arches that give distinction to the plaza side of the convento.

ARCADES

A conspicuous and certainly a characteristic feature of the missions was the arcade. Often there was an outer arcade as well as several inner ones. The long corridors across the front of such missions as San Fernando, San Miguel,

Purísima, Santa Inés, and Santa Barbara, are typical. Similar corridors surrounded the inner patios: some, as at San Juan Capistrano and San Luis Rey, were rather extensive. The corridor at San Gabriel, constructed in 1804 but since destroyed, was almost 350 feet long. At San Juan Capistrano the corridors totaled more than 600 feet. The immense inner court at San Luis Rey was enclosed by similar arcaded corridors. The front corridor of the convento at Santa Inés was originally 310 feet long. At San Antonio the front corridor was only about 227 feet long, but its arches were more uniform than most and were of almost perfect curvature. These arcades, or "cloisters," afforded a means of intercommunication between the different parts of the compound; they were dry during the rains and cool during the hot summers. Across the fronts of the buildings, these covered walkways similarly protected the lower floors of the convento from the occasional heavy rains. In general, only the church building was of stone; the other structures were of adobe, with brick only in the arches and round the doorways and on the piers.

The pillars supporting these arches varied considerably from mission to mission. Generally they were constructed of brick and were from three to five feet thick. Often they were set on bases; sometimes they had chamfered corners (as at Purísima). As a rule they were square, or nearly so. In some there was an ornamental ledge circling round the column just below the point from which the arch sprung.

The arches in these arcades usually were Roman: half round, or nearly so. Often there was variation; sometimes a series of perfectly sprung arches, then one, or two, flatter or wider ones. At San Miguel, for instance, there is considerable variance in the width of the arches. Immediately next to the church was an entrance in the wall connecting the convento to the church. It was, to judge from old photographs, wide enough to admit passage of a wagon. Next to it on the left were two more lintels supported by piers, then a low arch followed by four arches of equal span, and two wider arches. Thus the arcade was in no sense a continuous series of similar spans. There are thirteen piers supporting arches; the two end ones are smaller than the others. This corridor is 279 feet long from the wall of the church to the end. At San Juan Bautista there are two similar wide openings spanned by heavy lintels in place of arches; one is very near the left end of the corridor, the other is near the opposite end. Spanning the far end of this corridor is an extremely wide and flat arch that springs from the convento wall. Usually this wide space was spanned by heavy timbers.

There were no Gothic arches nor Mudejar arches in these corridors. Nor were the pillars very tall. Occasionally the molding and the chamfered corners were colored a dark red. Where no arches were used and simple post-and-lintel construction supported the overhangs, the posts were either of squared wooden beams or of adobes. The wooden posts often were capped with corbels to support the roof stringers. These adobes by their very nature did not allow of any ornament in the form of carving or molding. Only at Santa Inés, San Luis Rey, and San Juan Capistrano were there arcaded corridors along the inner patios of the original buildings. Generally these corridors were of one story, with flat roofs that often had a balustrade of ladrillos set in an openwork pattern, at the top.

BELFRIES

Perhaps the most distinctive feature, next to the red-tiled roofs, is the mission belfry. There are three general types: the campanario, the tower, and the primitive form. This last was merely a bell support consisting of two vertical posts surmounted by a heavy crossbeam, from which the bell was suspended. A belfry of this crude type was used for years at San Miguel; it was just to the left of the front entrance to the church. In 1911 a hideous steel tower, not unlike an oil derrick, was erected as bell tower. San Juan Bautista did not have a belfry of any kind until after the mission period when, during restoration, the wall joining the convento to the church was pierced and a bell was hung in the arch. A monstrous wooden belfry was erected in this same location in the late 1890's.

As soon as it was possible, the padres constructed more suitable and attractive belfries. The earlier churches probably had variants of the espadaña: a thick wall, with a roughly triangular or semicircular top, which gives height to the façade. It is not the same as the campanario, which usually—although not always—is separate from the church building. In some of the sixteenth-century fortress-style churches in Mexico there often was a small campanario atop one corner of the massive building. It is conceivable that the campanario was a step toward the true bell tower, at least economically; it obviously was less costly than the tower to construct and could, if properly engineered, be of considerable height.

THE ESPADAÑA

Since the *espadaña* often served as both a decorative architectural feature and as a belfry, its characteristics will be considered. The espadaña is a form of raised gable end of a church building; the Spanish word denotes a belfry of only one wall. However, in the colonial churches all espadañas are not belfries, nor are they pierced. This terraced, curved, and decorated front end of the church building is a marked characteristic of Spanish colonial architecture. The device of extending upward the gabled or pedimented façade of a church was employed to give added height and impressiveness to an otherwise rather low elevation; it is believed to have been employed originally as a means of lessening the risk of damage by earthquakes, for high naves in larger churches were subject to such damage. This characteristic decorative device is almost unprecedented in Spain, where earthquakes are not so common. Since these espadañas were rather thin, single-wall constructions, they are similar to the stepped gable fronts of houses found in the Low Countries, especially in Flanders and Holland. Their appearance in colonial architecture possibly can be traced to the influx of German and Flemish architects into the Span-

Fig. 5. The Espadañas at Monterey, San Diego, San Luis Rey.

ish colonies in the seventeenth century, when the form first made its appearance. Combined with other classical and baroque forms, the espadaña was a typical variation of the late Spanish Renaissance, and during the late baroque period assumed great decorative importance. In most of the California missions the espadaña is a conspicuous feature. Some, as in the rather small, stepped form at Santa Barbara, are very simple. Others, as at San Luis Rey, Carmel, and San Diego, are more elaborate. It is probable that the façade at Mission San Diego at one time had a good deal more ornament extending upward into the espadaña. Old photographs reveal traces of architectural and sculptured ornamentation that is barely indicated in the restoration. The cemetery wall gateway abutting the church of San Luis Rey is an example of the espadaña transplanted to the ground and out of context. The richly decorated espadaña at the Capilla Real in Monterey has already been discussed.

THE CAMPANARIO

Strictly speaking, the campanario is a bell tower. However, there is a distinction between the true tower of several stories and the single-walled, often detached structure raised primarily to hold bells. Both types exist in the Cali-

Fig. 6. The Campanarios at San Gabriel and Santa Inés.

fornia missions. The best examples are the campanarios at Mission Santa Inés and Mission San Gabriel. The restored campanarios at San Diego and Purísima are also good examples. They differ from the terraced bell towers in that they are merely pierced walls, varying in height and in their position with regard to the church building.

Although the design and disposition of these belfries are characteristic of the California missions, there are similar examples in Mexico. The most striking belfry of this type is that of the church known as the Sanctuary of Guadalupe in Guadalajara, which might have served at least as an inspiration. It is probable that Father José María Zalvidea, in charge of Mission San Gabriel from 1808 to 1826, was responsible for the construction of its campanario. The original belfry of that mission, which was at the northeast corner of the church and was called an espadaña in the mission report, was destroyed by the 1812 earthquake and was never rebuilt. Unlike the belfries at the other missions, that at San Gabriel was placed at the rear of the church, its wall joining the last of the heavy buttresses. The design is irregular and as a result is all the more picturesque. The left side is marked by three "steps," which begin high up and are followed by a graceful inward curve leading to another and smaller step on which rests the capping arch. Only this upward curve is repeated on the opposite side; the bottom of the curve continues as a straight line to join the buttress. There are six arched spaces each of a size to correspond with the size of the bell hung in it. Uppermost is a small arched opening; below, on a line, are three of equal height, though the one on the right is considerably wider than the others; and below this row are two more openings, the one on the right a bit larger than those above. The largest arch occupies the lower left area. Architectural moldings of brick—double and triple ledges that project slightly—form bands along the edges of the steps and carry the architectural line to the adjacent church. There are now four bells hanging in the arches. A beautiful wrought-iron cross surmounts the topmost arch.

Most closely resembling the San Gabriel campanario is that of Santa Inés. Both Father Calzada and Father Uría of Santa Inés had served at San Gabriel, and it is possible that the campanario at San Gabriel served as the model for the later one at Santa Inés. Indeed, the two missions are very similar. The campanario has the same position relative to the church as did the destroyed tower at San Gabriel.

The Santa Inés campanario was originally of brick and adobe, and abutted the church on the north side, so that there was a continuous wall surface. This campanario was probably completed at the same time as the church, in 1817. Because of neglect and deterioration, it collapsed during a heavy rain storm early in 1911. The following year it was somewhat redesigned and was rebuilt of concrete. Unfortunately, the awkward massiveness of the reconstruction, with its extra arches for bells, marred the character of the whole. During extensive renovation and repair of the mission in 1947–1948, the campanario was again rebuilt. The original design and character were restored, although the concrete with its simulated adobe-surfaced texture does not entirely succeed in continuing the character of the church with its buttressed walls and fine-crackled surface texture.

Whether the façade of Mission Dolores (San Francisco de Asís) can rightly be called a campanario is questionable, but since the mission had neither a tower nor a separate campanario, it could be called one. In the upper part of the façade there are three openings; the two side ones are arched, the center one is rectangular. The bells were hung in these openings. The present deeply overhanging roof was not the original one; for what appears to be truncated pillars were piers that extended above the roof line and terminated in finials. With these the upper part of the façade had much more the character of a campanario. Apart from the roof, there has been very little change or restoration. The façade is very different from those of the other missions and has an unusual distinction.

In one sense, the façade of San Luis Obispo is also a campanario. This narthex, or porch, bearing three arched openings above, is a recent and fairly accurate restoration. A sketch by Edward Vischer made between 1860 and 1870 shows three arched doorways in the front, and above these three somewhat smaller arches in which bells are hanging. There are also two arches on a line with these on the north (right) side. Apparently the entire upper part over the entrance served as a very large "porch," on the walls of which were the arches containing the bells. In the normal church of this type the choir occupied this space. The roof of the church was continuous and there was no break; the bell front was not an espadaña. The same drawing shows two fairly low windows on the north (right) wall of the nave. Unlike that of Mission Dolores, this façade-camparanio has no architectural or sculptural ornamentation whatever. Much the same situation obtains at Mission San Antonio de Padua. Here the narthex wall becomes the true façade of the church: the base has three arches. Above the arched entrance is perhaps the most individual campanario of all. It is constructed of brick and resembles in form a baroque espadaña with a large arched opening in the center. Flanking this on each side, at the bottom of the "gable," is a low tower pierced with an arch. The bells hung in these three arches. The entire front has recently been restored and now presents the richness of the original. This campanario is not so high as that of Santa Inés and San Gabriel, but it is architecturally more elegant. The apex is crowned by a pyramid surmounted by a beautiful wrought-iron cross. Each of the three arches has a small wooden balustrade.

After the great earthquake in 1812 that destroyed San Juan Capistrano, the largest church in California, a kind of campanario was evolved there. The great tower had collapsed. The bells that had hung in the tower were placed in four deep arches which pierced the wall connecting the church with an adjacent building. It is not, of course, a true campanario, and there is nothing architecturally distinctive about it.

Originally, the low tower of Nuestra Señora de Los Angeles (the Plaza church) was topped by a companario having one small arch and two large ones. The design was extremely simple: the curved top of the campanario was flanked by one step on each side. Whether or not the base of the southwest tower at San Luis Rey was to have supported a matching tower or a campanario is not clear. An early drawing shows the mission with both towers complete;

the project, however, was never carried out. The baptistery occupies the base of the unfinished tower.

The original design of the belfry at the Capilla Real, and the one actually built, called for a campanario with two arches or openings for bells. The base was simple, pierced with a small square window. The campanario projected forward from the façade wall and was of fair thickness. The present bell tower of one story is almost an exact replica of the campanario except that it is now four-sided and there is a pyramidal tile-covered capping surmounting it, each side duplicating the original design. The two arches on the face were very simple; above them, below a plain cornice, were two strips of narrow molding. In the center was a curving, triangular form capped by a finial, extending upward perhaps eight feet. A simple finial was at the outer edges. In the 1850's three bells hung in the arches: a large one on the right and two smaller ones, one above the other, in the left arch. A fourth bell hung from a wooden frame attached to the rear of the left arch.

It becomes apparent that the height and elaborateness of the campanario was conditioned by the ever-present scarcity of funds and materials. Since most of these structures were made of adobe, any great height was not feasible without adequate buttressing, and heavy buttressing would have spoiled the design. Nor was it feasible to work details into the adobe. As in the espadaña, architectural or sculptural ornament, if there was any in the campanario, was executed in brick.

TOWERS

More picturesque and certainly more spectacular than the campanarios are the mission bell towers. What gives them their monumental character is their mass and bulk. They are unlike the towers of the Texas missions, which are more ornate. They are peculiar to California, lacking, as they do, some of the refinements of their Mexican prototypes. Most of these towers are three-storied and are capped by a hemispherical dome. The heavy base of masonry is generally windowless, or at best has only a small, high-placed opening. As a rule, the squared base of the tower is of nearly solid construction, with a filling of rubble. In some missions, however, the base of the tower served as a space for the baptistery, or, as at Santa Barbara, it contained a narrow "winding" staircase leading to the upper tiers.

All the towers are terraced—typical of many Spanish colonial churches. But the California towers are much simpler, and for the most part they are not nearly so tall as either the Mexican or the Texan towers. Generally there is no ornament except a decorative molding projecting cornice-like at the top of each terrace, or story. Usually the tower base is the same height as the walls of the church; sometimes it is a bit higher. The second story is stepped back, with a full arched opening on all four sides. The Santa Barbara towers are slightly chamfered at the four corners. The tower at Mission San Buenaventura has ornamental finials capping the four corners of the second and third tier. The third tier is slightly smaller than the second and has a similar arrangement. A curious deviation exists in the San Buenaventura tower: the two upper tiers are not centered over the heavy base. The reason for this is that the tower was rebuilt after the earthquakes of 1812, and the base was then much enlarged to serve as buttress for the façade, which it overlapped. The tower of Mission San Luis Rey above the wall height is almost octagonal, so sharply cut are the corners. The surmounting dome is an irregular octagon, with a small square lantern at the very top. It is the best of the towers in the classical style. This tower, that of San Buenaventura, and those of Santa Barbara are similar.

The domed tower of Carmel Mission is distinctive, and though not so soaring as the other mission towers, it is richer and more satisfying architecturally. It (the left tower) is short and rather squat and is topped by an ornamental molding which, like the others, is rather classical in style. The second tier again departs from the uniform. It has two arches on the façade, or front, and also at the back, but only one arch on the side. A molding breaks the vertical line at the point where the two arches spring. This tier has a very elaborate finial at each corner. Above it is a rather low octagonal drum that supports the unusual dome, which is virtually egg-shaped in contrast to the half-round dome of the other missions. Surmounting the dome is a finial topped by a wrought-iron cross. The whole quality of this tower, and for that matter the façade, is strongly baroque or, more correctly, Mudejar. Almost all the ruined details have been restored. The base of the tower is occupied by the baptistery. Access to the upper tier is by means of an exterior stone stairway. The second (or right) tower, differs from its opposite in that it is smaller and the second tier has only one arch, lacks the decorative finials, and has a low dome base surmounted by a finial bearing a cross. Apparently the dome was never finished. In both towers the arches are on the three sides away from the church; the curved pediment of the espadaña and its contiguous supporting wall extend up to the second tier, thereby blocking the arch. Had this church been built in Mexico, the dome would have been covered with *azulejos*. It contrasts admirably with the tall, more graceful, and more classic towers of Mission Santa Barbara. There the domes, like those at San Luis Rey and San Buenaventura, are capped by small lanterns. Access to the very top of the tower domes was by means of tile or brick steps along one quadrant of the dome.

There were towers also at Santa Cruz, San José, Santa Clara, San Fernando, and San Juan Capistrano. The great tower at San Juan Capistrano fell during the earthquake of 1812. According to tradition it was high enough (120 feet) to be seen for miles. Unlike the towers of the other missions, it was placed directly over the center of the church entrance. The base was very massive, and the entire structure was of stone. It had two terraces similar to the one at Mission San Luis Rey.

THE CHURCH NAVE

There are several fundamental and necessary areas of activity which must be provided for in each church. Reduced to the barest essentials, all the activities could be housed in one single room, which is precisely what obtained in the very first chapels. The sanctuary is necessary of course. This is the separated area in which the altar is placed and which generally is set apart by means of a railing or division of some kind; it is usually three steps above the floor level of the nave. A sacristy, or vestry, is a necessary room, accessible from the sanctuary, in which the vestments are kept and in which the priest prepares himself for the service. There must be space for those participating in the service, and this area is determined by the size of the community of worshipers. Necessary also, is a place, usually near the entrance to the church, for the baptismal font. In larger churches there may be a separate room for this. Originally, in the early church, the baptistery was housed outside the church proper in a separate building. Some churches also have a mortuary or funerary chapel. Provision is invariably made, even in small churches, for as many secondary or side altars as are deemed necessary by the needs of the community.

As the population of a mission grew, the size and the arrangement of the church plan changed. Yet in plan, the mission churches were consistently simple. As previously pointed out, the single-aisled plan resulted largely from structural limitations. Had it been possible to add lateral aisles, an interesting construction problem would have presented itself. This is precisely what occurred at San Juan Bautista. All but three of the mission churches are of the single-nave or single-aisle type with no transept.

The three churches having the essentials of a cruciform plan are San Luis Rey, San Juan Bautista, and the ruined San Juan Capistrano. The large cruciform churches in Mexico and elsewhere generally have transept entrances at the ends of the arms. The California churches are not truly cruciform; they are, rather, single-nave churches with deep bays at the transepts and no entrances there.

In most of the mission churches the roof or ceiling is flat. In some the beams are exposed, in others they are hidden by a ceiling. In the recent restoration at San Buenaventura the wooden ceiling was removed and the old vigas thus were exposed. The lighting by means of windows is also consistent: all nave windows are high in the walls. In the New Mexico pueblo churches additional light was brought into the sanctuary by means of a transverse clerestory window, the ceiling of the sanctuary being higher than that of the nave. This window was not more than two or three feet high and usually extended the

width of the nave. The California churches have no clerestory window, probably because they have correspondingly larger windows not only in the nave
but usually in the sanctuary also, where as a rule there is at least one window.
Consèquently, in nearly all the missions, the sanctuary is rather dimly lighted.

The position of the sacristy in relation to the sanctuary varies; likely enough,
expediency was an important factor in determining their position. In the remodeling or rebuilding of a mission the position as well as the appearance of
these rooms has sometimes been changed. The present sacristy at Santa Barbara is not the original one, which was a large room to the left of the sanctuary;
in remodeling the mission an addition was made at the rear, extending the
full width of the church. Entrance to the sacristy is through a door in the
reredos wall, the door being concealed from view by the altar, which stands
free. Several missions have sacristies at the rear and are entered from the sanctuary through a door, or a pair of doors, in the reredos wall (San Diego, San
Gabriel, San Fernando, San Luis Obispo, Santa Inés, Santa Barbara). The
others have their sacristies to the right or left of the building; generally these
are housed in a structure of the lean-to type and often are an addition to rather
than an integral original part of the larger structure.

Several of the churches had separate baptisteries, but only in their later
buildings. Traditionally the baptistery is near the front of the church. In some
missions it was in the base of one of the towers: at San Luis Rey, San Diego,
San Fernando, Carmel, San Juan Bautista, it was on the left; at Santa Barbara
the baptistery is now in the base of the right tower. The San Gabriel baptistery
is in the original mortuary chapel opening off the nave on the right. In the
other churches, where there is no separate room, a baptismal font is placed in
a niche when one is available (as at Santa Inés), or in a corner near the front
entrance. At San Buenaventura the original room to the left has been restored.

The plan of a few churches deviated from the narrow, unbroken nave by
having side chapels. The deep side chapels at San Luis Rey have been mentioned. This church has, in addition, a large separate mortuary chapel, which
will be described later. At San Juan Bautista the two bays near the sanctuary,
which give an almost cruciform arrangement to the nave, are actually spaces
left open when the plan to have three aisles was abandoned. In the church at
Santa Barbara there are two distinct side chapels opposite each other near the
front of the church. These contain side altars and are still used as originally
planned.

It is clear, then, that expediency, the nature of materials, and cost and labor
factors influenced the plan of the churches. Although in several later buildings
stone was substituted for the earlier adobe, the same general proportions were
observed. Both the adobe and the stone available made the construction of
very thick walls almost mandatory. These thick walls, especially if they were
constructed of adobe and were to be rather high, called for the use of but-

tresses. The bulk, height, and spacing of these, whether they were made of adobe, brick, or stone, have given to the church buildings distinctive characteristics. Often the buttress emphasizes the sturdy, fortress-like character of the mission. In the New Mexico pueblo churches brick was not so commonly used, and there the buttress was generally low and extremely massive. It is probable that the pitched roof, which exerts a strong lateral thrust, called for the use of a buttress of the taller California type. The frequency of earthquakes was another factor that prompted the use of buttresses. The north wall of the church at San Buenaventura has no buttresses, however, although the tower has two. Examination of old photographs of Missions San Diego, San Luis Rey, Santa Clara, San Antonio, and San Miguel reveals no buttressing.

Most of the buttresses are merely braces. Some, as at Santa Inés, are huge rectangular masses rounded somewhat at the top. Those at San Gabriel are not only functional but beautifully constructed and topped with decorative finials. On the north wall of Carmel Mission six clean-cut buttresses rise from the thickened base of the wall, and between them are spaces for windows. In addition, there are three short auxiliary braces of stone. Whether these smoothly finished vertical buttresses were originally decorated at their caps, it is impossible to know. In any event, they create a very attractive pattern and, like the buttresses of San Gabriel, give to the wall a pronounced fortress-like appearance.

Buttresses were often placed elsewhere than on the side walls. The diagonal finlike braces at the front corners of Mission San Diego are conspicuous. A similar but less attractive mass was placed at the left corner of San Buenaventura; at Santa Barbara there is one bracing the left tower. Where there were none—or only small ones—along the walls, the corners were usually reinforced, as at Mission Dolores. Just how much support these reinforcements gave the structure, it is difficult to tell. But they often add distinction to an otherwise uninteresting building. The towers, campanario, side chapels, and other adjacent structures also acted as buttresses. Since the buttress was certainly not very effective protection from earthquake damage, it has been suggested that its continued use was a survival not only of the fortress church of sixteenth-century Mexico but of the architecture of the Middle Ages in Spain and southern France.

For the most part, pilasters on the interior corresponded to the buttresses on the exterior side walls. These pilasters, which often were decorated, tended to break the long wall surfaces of the nave into sections that afforded the opportunity of creating side chapels. In some, as at San Miguel, the pilaster emphasized the extensive decorations on the walls and created the illusion that the church was larger than it actually was.

The most elaborate existing mission church is that of San Luis Rey. Its construction was begun in 1811 under the direction of Father Peyri, and it was completed in 1815. (The dome over the crossing was finished in 1829.) The nave is about 164 feet long and slightly more than 27 feet wide. The "transept" arms are short—about 15½ feet deep—but are nearly 25 feet wide. Each has a neoclassic side altar. The long nave is divided into five "bays" by pilasters. The sacristy (28 by 19 ft.) is to the right (north) of the sanctuary and is entered from it. On the opposite side is a second large room used as a choir. Each room has a small altar. The unusual feature of the San Luis Rey nave is the elaborate mortuary chapel on the north side—an octagonal room opening from the nave. Opposite the entrance is a small rectangular recess in which stands an altar of neoclassic style in a tiny sanctuary. Both the chapel and the small sanctuary have domed roofs made of brick. From the chapel a door leads directly into the cemetery. The pillars, altar, altar reredos, and relief ornament are of brick and plaster. Like the nave, the chapel is lighted by windows placed high on the wall. The chapel has one other interesting feature: on each side of the little sanctuary is a very narrow doorway leading to a flight of steps that terminates in a lookout behind and above the altar. Opposite the entrance to the mortuary chapel is an arched doorway leading from the nave into a small patio. The curvature of the arch is almost strictly Mudejar. The doorway is one of the best examples of this type in California.

Directly over the entrance to the nave is the choir, apparently supported by a huge decorative arch that spans the width of the nave. It is the vigas, however, which actually support the choir. Entrance to the baptistery in the base of the unfinished tower is to the left, under the choir. On the opposite side of the nave is a doorway leading to the steps which ascend to the choir and, higher up, to the bell tower and the roof. The most spectacular feature of the nave, however, is the dome over the crossing. The original dome was smaller than the present one, which is a "restoration" dating from the 1890's. The first dome was lower and could not be seen from the outside. The base, or drum, for the dome is octagonal and its sides are pierced by windows that give light to the transept area. The nave differs from the usual nave in that the floor of the sanctuary, raised the traditional three steps above the nave floor, is continuous with those of the two adjoining side chapels. It is further lighted by windows placed high along both walls.

Although the San Juan Capistrano church is a romantic ruin, some description of its nave is of interest. Undoubtedly this was the grandest of all the mission churches. It was constructed almost entirely of sandstone; this was of two kinds, both fine-grained. One kind, a blue-gray, was used for detail work and for support around windows and doors. The other, yellow, was used in major parts of the structure, where it was supplemented by tile and brick.

The stone church was begun early in 1797 and was completed in 1806. Somewhat like that of San Luis Rey, the building is in the form of a Latin cross, 180 feet long and 30 feet wide. The transept arms were not equal: the eastern arm was slightly more than 19 feet long, the western almost 22 feet. Over the entrance end was the tallest tower in California. The baptistery was on the right side at the place where in the other missions the tower stands. It was entered by means of a door leading off the nave. Another door, directly opposite, opened on the plaza. Deviating from the usual plan, the church did not form a corner of the compound but projected considerably into what was then a plaza.

Unlike the other churches, San Juan Capistrano was roofed with shallow *bóvedas* (domes); of the original seven, only the *bóveda* spanning the sanctuary still stands. In the treatment of the roof, even in the simple vaulting, the church resembled some of the early Augustinian churches in Mexico. According to reports, there was a cupola dome over the crossing at the transept.

In front of the transept the nave is divided into two nearly square bays. Instead of the customary pilasters extending to the ceiling, formerly there were arches spanning the length of the nave and springing from rather short piers, or pilasters. This broke the nave into round-headed niches. Similarly, transverse arches spanned the nave and supported the low *bóvedas* that made up the roof. The dome over the sanctuary was groined and was further supported by very shallow arches embedded in the wall. Separating the sanctuary from the nave proper was another great arch, somewhat in the tradition of fourteenth-century Italian churches. The entire vaulting and the engaged arches along the walls resembled the architecture of the early Mexican churches more markedly than do those of the other missions.

As in other churches, the windows were high on the walls. The sacristy occupied the northwest corner formed by the cruciform shape of the church and was entered by a door from the left transept. In general, the walls were somewhat thicker than common, so as to accommodate various niches for the placing of statuary. In the wall at the back of the sanctuary were three tiers of three arches: nine niches to provide for the reredos sculptures. All this was of stone, with very carefully cut borders and decorative moldings.

Another mission having an unusual—that is, a different—nave was San Juan Bautista. The church was planned to have three aisles to accommodate an anticipated large neophyte attendance. The plan is now cruciform. The original two side aisles were a change from the conventional single nave of 10 varas width. The present side walls of the nave were originally brick arches springing from piers. These arches have long since been filled in with adobe brick. The original side aisles were thus closed off, but the two bays, or niches, nearest the sanctuary were left open, giving to the church its cruciformity. Had the arches not been filled in, the mission would have been the widest church in the Californias and the only one having three aisles. At the front, on the left of the nave, is the almost square baptistery, and directly opposite was formerly a room or chapel that may have been used for funeral services. The reredos back of the main altar was two-tiered, with six niches for the sculptures. The center niche has a beautiful Mudejar arch. As in San Juan Capistrano, an arch spans the nave, separating the transept from the rest of the church. The original sacristy was a very large room in the north (right) angle of the transept; the present sacristy is on the opposite side of the sanctuary. For years there was a flat ceiling of boards fastened to the under side of the vigas and cutting across the arch spanning the nave. In the center of the ceiling was painted the face of Christ, and there was a wide, rather plain border that acted as a frame. When the church was restored this ceiling was removed, exposing the vigas. Unfortunately, the walls had become so weakened that it was necessary to span the nave with secondary beams half way between the high-placed square windows and the tops of the arches. The entire architectural beauty and the feeling of spaciousness have been destroyed. The original outer walls of adobe have for the most part crumbled away or are in very poor condition. A clumsy system of concrete braces has been erected to prevent collapse of these walls. These braces are completely out of scale and destroy the beauty of the bare adobe walls.

San Carlos (Carmel) Mission has been much restored. The structure was typical. It was built of stone between 1793 and 1797. Its nave was very long (150 ft.) and narrow (29 ft.). The walls are not as high as in other churches. A short distance within the church, to the left, a beautiful doorway opens into a side chapel of rather large proportions. The sacristy is to the right of the sanctuary, and opening off it there is a small chamber with a stairway leading to the pulpit. Access to the pulpit was through a doorway cut into the wall.

The original ceiling of the Carmel church was the most unusual in California. The nave was partitioned into bays of almost equal size by pilasters somewhat Doric in style. From these piers, which continued the curve, sprang stone arches. This catenated arch structure was not evident from the outside, since a low-pitched gable roof covered it. Actually, the walls of the nave curve outward somewhat near the top, resulting in an almost elliptical inside ceiling. The roof collapsed in 1852. Heavy buttresses carried the weight through to the exterior.

The baptistery, to the left of the entrance, occupies the base of the tower and is approximately ten feet square; however, it is actually octagonal, for the corners of the room have been cut off.

In San Gabriel the more conventional plan was followed, with a sacristy behind the sanctuary and under the same roof. Originally, when the campanario was standing, the room on the ground floor probably served as the baptistery. The baptistery now occupies a chapel that is entered from about the middle of the nave, and which at one time was probably the mortuary chapel, since it is fairly close to the door leading to the cemetery. Nearly opposite is a very wide double door, which now leads to the street. The walls are high and very thick. A door opened from the south wall of the sacristy into what was originally the inner patio, the arrangement being very similar to that at Santa Inés. The south door of the nave has on the outside a sculptural decoration with a niche for a statue. The style is reminiscent of Mexican plateresque.

The nave of San Fernando Rey is 154 feet long and 25 feet wide; it has very thick walls that taper slightly toward the top. The belfry, or bell tower, was on the right of the entrance; on the ground floor was a room containing the stairway. Opposite it is the baptistery. The sacristy is at the end of the church; entrance from the sanctuary is by means of two doors, one on each side of the altar. From the sacristy a door on the south side led to the patios. Not quite in the middle of the church are two doors: the one on the north (left) side opened into the cemetery; the other, opposite, opens into the patio. The ceiling is flat, as in most missions that have simple naves, and is carried on heavy vigas. The ends are supported by large decorated corbels. Between the piers that continue from the outside buttresses there are slight indentations in the walls, serving somewhat as rudimentary bays. The tops of these are arched. Most of the windows on the north wall of the nave, and several on the south wall, have been blocked in. But in the interior the outlines of these windows have been painted with dark lines so as to emphasize the depth of the resulting niche. The effect is very curious.

Quite similar is the Santa Barbara nave, now almost completely restored. In plan the Santa Barbara church is typical: the long, narrow nave, the slightly raised sanctuary at the west end, the sacristy behind it (a later addition, for the original sacristy opened off to the south, left, side). The church is 163 feet long and 27½ feet wide. There are two small side chapels, built into and through the walls, a short distance from the entrance. These have domed ceilings decorated with painted coffers. Near the sanctuary are doors; the one on the right (north) side leads, up a flight of steps, to the cemetery. The one opposite opens into the inner patio, or cloister. Here the windows are of more interesting design. Distinctly Moorish in style, they cut through the six-foot stone walls and are splayed to give more light. The walls are divided into sections by flat pilasters. So much restoration was done after the 1925 earthquake and in 1950 that only the basic plan and the window styles of the original remain. At present the baptistery occupies the base of the north tower. The ceiling of the nave itself is flat.

The nave of San Antonio de Padua has the distinction of possessing a narthex covered by a vault. It is almost a half circle and extends from near the floor to the ceiling. The nave proper seems wide because of the relatively low walls and the somewhat unusual roofing. The roof is actually supported by trusses on vigas spanning the nave. Instead of a flat ceiling nailed to the underside of the vigas, beams were fastened to form an angle between the wall and the ceiling. The upper ends of those beams abut the vigas at a point about one third their span out from the wall. These slanted into the wall. The entire frame was covered with boards; the result was a compromise between an arched or vaulted and a flat ceiling and had somewhat the appearance of a gambrel roof. This type of ceiling was common in many Spanish colonial churches and, especially in the Andean area, afforded a base for complicated patterns stemming from Mudejar designs.

A large transverse arch springing from piers at the sanctuary line separates the sanctuary from the nave. The face of the arch—that is, the spandrel—was decorated with stars, and the soffit, or underside, was painted to resemble courses of stone.

At the front of the church, the choir loft was reached by a stairway built outside the wall which formed part of the eastern end of the corridor of the convento. To allow for sufficient clearance, the roof of the convento was raised at that point.

The nave at San Luis Obispo somewhat resembles that of San Antonio, but only in that it has a narthex, or entrance. The sanctuary is at the opposite end of the long nave, and behind it is the sacristy, which originally consisted of two rooms and was somewhat wider than the church. The nave had only two windows on the left side and one on the right, although there was formerly an additional one in this wall. There appears to have been a narrow doorway leading from the sanctuary to the patio on the left. There were no side chapels. It is probable that the baptistery was placed to one side in the narthex, which has since been removed. The ceiling of the nave had an open-timber roof which has been partly restored. This mission church has probably undergone more rebuilding and restoration than any of the others. The wide side "chapel" to the right of the sanctuary is a modern addition; though it serves somewhat as one arm of a transept, it spoils the architectural simplicity of the church. The main reredos behind the altar is of late colonial style, almost severely neoclassic, as is a side altar on the left. It is of an extremely simple pediment type; a pedestal in the center supports the statue of the patron saint. Beyond the supporting decorative pillars there is a statuary niche on each side.

Certainly one of the most striking naves is that of Mission San Miguel, not because of its plan but because of the decorations, which have been described earlier. Structurally it has undergone few changes and, fortunately, with Santa Inés, remains very much as it was more than a century ago. The two churches are very similar: long, narrow naves of adobe walls with high-placed windows. The sacristy at San Miguel forms a wing off the sanctuary to the north (right) and projects into the cemetery. About halfway down this wall there is a niche that serves as a confessional. Originally it was used as a baptismal niche and had doors to close it when not in use. Opposite is the door leading into the convento area. The ceiling is of heavy vigas with fine corbels that in some places extend through the thick walls to the outside. The most spectacular part of the nave is the elaborate and somewhat garishly painted reredos of wood, with its ornate columns and pilasters and rich entablature. The sanctuary has curved stone steps leading up to it from the floor of the nave. The pulpit is on the right, and is well decorated, with an almost Mudejar baldachin. Sculptures for the side altars in and near the sanctuary are placed on pedestals against backgrounds painted to receive them, instead of in true niches.

The Capilla Real, or Presidio Church, in Monterey was not a mission church, although for a time it served as a chapel. The nave is of good proportions. The transept with its doors was added to the single nave in 1858, when the building was enlarged and much of it reconstructed. A drawing made before this time shows the nave with only one window on the southeast side, a rather small rectangle, very near the campanario. There was a sort of lean-to, very probably the sacristy, on the same side of the building, near or at the rear. It had two small round windows. The sanctuary had no window to light it, as it does now. If the drawing was at least fairly accurate, then radical changes were later made in both the plan and the elevation of the church. It is very likely that when the espadaña was converted into a tower in 1893 the original square or rectangular windows of the nave were converted to the pointed Gothic type (from the interior these still appear rectangular). At the same time, they were very much enlarged. The window over the front entrance illuminating the choir has a low, flat arch.

The interior, in contrast to the façade, lacks distinction. Unfortunately it has been almost totally modernized. Were it not for the old paintings of the Stations of the Cross and a few sculptures dating from the mission period, it would in no way resemble a mission church. There is now no semblance of "an elaborate reredos." In its place there is a niche about ten feet high with the outlines of a convoluted Mudejar arch, flanked by two small niches with roundheaded arches. There is no ornamentation of any kind on the walls or ceiling. The ceiling is made of tongue-and-groove boards apparently nailed to the underside of the vigas, for the old corbels still project from the walls. It is a small and unpretentious church, all its former official glory having been lost in the modernization.

THE CHOIR

A particularly important feature of the interior of all the mission churches is the choir. This area is invariably a porchlike structure extending from wall to wall, directly inside the entrance to the church. Usually, it is supported by rather large vigas. The means of access to the choir loft varied, although generally there was a stairway rising from the back of the church. In some—

Santa Barbara and San Luis Rey, for instance—entrance to the choir was also possible by means of a doorway leading from the second floor of the adjoining convento. San Juan Bautista and San Luis Rey also have stairs leading up to the choir that begin in a room to the right of the entrance; in Santa Barbara there is a stairway in the base of the left tower. A few once had outside stairways, such as the famous one at San Gabriel. The one at Santa Inés was completely incorporated into the wall when the church was enlarged; that at San Luis Rey still exists but the doorway has long since been closed off.

In several churches a rather dramatic character was given the space below the choir by a great arch spanning the back of the nave. As a rule, it was more decorative than structural, as at San Luis Rey. The spandrels and soffits were painted in the typical marbleized patterns that decorated other parts of the church. At San Miguel, to give greater pretentiousness to the choir, a painted balustrade on the side walls continued the choir railing. This was in imitation of many Spanish and Mexican churches, in which the choir frequently took on a U, or horseshoe, shape, extending along the sides. At Santa Inés the choir has an architectural false front of several arches painted on canvas and mounted on light wooden frames attached to the railing.

The size and depth of the choir quite logically varied with the size and importance of the church. An organ was usually placed near the window. This window, which as a rule was not very large and conformed with the external decoration of the façade, was generally the only means of natural illumination.

In the California missions there were no choir stalls, though almost every Mexican church has such stalls. There were two reasons for their absence. The first was that there was no company of priests or brothers to recite in unison the various offices of the day. Second, there were too few skilled craftsmen to create anything more than basic necessities. The carvers were put to work on confessionals, doors, chairs, and benches, where they were most needed and, understandably, where the carvings would be seen by all. Undoubtedly the choir stall would have become a part of the architectural decoration of the church had the mission continued to grow. In the choir there was no carving, no ornamentation except the painting that was continuous from the ceiling and walls of the church proper. Invariably the floor of the choir was of wood and was all of one level; later remodeling for greater suitability to the purposes has introduced a stepped floor so that the space next to the façade wall is several feet higher than that at the railing. This makes the window appear to be almost at floor level.

SCULPTURAL DECORATIONS

The sculptural decorations of the mission churches are not so conspicuous a feature of the architecture as they are in their Mexican prototypes. At first glance there appears to be none to speak of. Yet in nearly all the extant churches there are evidences of some decoration. Probably because of the lack of trained native sculptors, or the absence of the *tallador* and, above all, lack of funds for the commissioning of such works until late in the period, there is comparatively little. Most of what little remains is of dubious artistic merit. Much of this has been called "Indian" carving. Unquestionably, most of the stone and wood carving was executed by Indians; but in almost all of it the designs, patterns, and the total effect can be directly traced to classical and Mudejar origins. Architectural details were gleaned and copied from books, and it is reasonable to assume that similar works were the source of the sculptured architectural decorations. There is nothing to compare with the elaborate doorway of the now-ruined Mission San José de Aguayo in San Antonio, Texas, or with San Xavier del Bac near Tucson.

There are three broad groups into which the sculpture can be divided. In the first group are the decorations on the façade of the church. Most of these are in relief or, as at Santa Barbara, in the round. There, on the original façade, which collapsed during the earthquake in 1925, stood three sandstone figures, a little less than life size, representing Faith, Hope, and Charity. Although in their manner of execution and style these statues have a pronounced archaic appearance and it is generally conceded that they were the work of Indian craftsmen, the models were distinctly classical in type. The technique was determined by the character of the material—a fairly fine sandstone from the neighboring mountains. When the figures fell from their places atop the pediment they were broken, and only fragments remain. They have been replaced by modern figures that stylistically have no relation to the missions.

Few of the missions had freestanding sculpture on the exterior. At San Luis Rey there is a niche on each side of the entrance from which the original statues have long since disappeared. They were probably of stone; two modern brick and mortar figures now occupy the niches. The nearest approach to similar freestanding figures is the figure of the Virgin, not unlike the Virgin of Guadalupe, over the entrance to the Capilla Real in Monterey. The carving shows fairly good workmanship and gives this façade (which dates from 1794) the distinction of being the most elaborate in California. The work must have been done under the supervision of the now-famous master, Manuel Estevan Ruíz.

Over the side (now street) entrance to the San Gabriel church there is a deep niche; a modern figure, probably representing Junípero Serra with his Indian boy, occupies the place. At San Buenaventura, over the side door, there is a small niche that at one time was a place for a figure. Although there is no substantiating evidence, it is probable that there was decorative sculpture on the façade of the San Juan Capistrano church that was destroyed. The elaborateness of the decorative stone treatment of remaining interior arches and columns suggests similar embellishment on the outside.

Whether or not the old church of Santa Clara had sculptures in niches or on pedestals on each side and above the entrance is not known. The widely reproduced painting (dated 1849) of the façade shows three such statues. However, since the architectural details were painted on the façade rather than sculptured as at Santa Barbara, it is probable that these figures were also painted. In any event, they were intended to have the effect of sculpture. The modern chapel, which is an adapted "reconstruction" somewhat enlarged, has all the features of the original duplicated in relief and in the round, though the details show many changes.

The second kind of sculptural decoration is that generally found as relief carvings on columns, pilasters, arches, capitals, and panels. There is virtually no decoration of this sort in the missions. At best there is fluting or an occasional leaf or plant form cut into the stone. The most elaborate carving of this type can still be seen in the arches and capitals of the sanctuary of San Juan Capistrano. At San Luis Rey some very fine work in brick and mortar is to be seen in the mortuary chapel, over the altar. The detail work of the columns, their Ionic capitals, the friezes, and other details of the classical pediment is perhaps the best extant in the missions.

Strictly speaking, the distinction between architectural detail, such as moldings, and decorative sculpture is difficult to make. If one is searching for leaf and figure patterns, for arabesques in wood, stone, or stucco such as commonly cover large areas of the Mexican *fachada* or the ceilings of apses or chapels, then there is nothing comparable to be found in California. The principal ornamental devices are the decorative moldings that run along façades, across the tops of pillars or at their bases. These invariably were made of burned bricks the thickness of which varied somewhat. The moldings served as a unifying element in the over-all design. Moldings certainly affect the appearance of a building. Those found in the missions are generally of classic style and have little variety of form. Because of the character of the material used, the moldings are strong rather than delicate. Again, the finest examples are to be found in the ruins of San Juan Capistrano. In contrast to those at San Luis Rey, which are "carved" from ladrillos, they are of stone and hence are more delicate.

The use of finials at the corners of towers and at the tops of buttresses (as at San Gabriel) varied. Some were pyramidal, ornamental variations of the fortress style of *almenas*. Others, especially on the towers, were in the form of small urns. There was little if any decoration such as the traditional Roman garland on these. When the finials were used in the interior, as in the old reredos at Santa Barbara and San Miguel, these urns, or finials, were painted either on wood or on canvas. No example of carved ornament in the interior of a mission church is known, except those on later wood reredos.

Occasionally the keystones of stone arches were carved with simple designs. San Juan Capistrano Mission has several of these; one design is an eight-petaled, starlike flower set in a rhomboidal frame bordered by scallops, making an extremely simple but effective design. Notwithstanding that most of such work was executed by Indians, the designs on the whole hark back to the classic and many of them to Mudejar. There were numerous variations of the basic rosette design, and in some missions the keystone as well as the voussoirs were merely channeled or grooved. At San Gabriel there is a six-pointed star enclosed in a square with another star suspended below it. These are carved in low relief, rather than incised. Such ornament was possible only in stone or very hard-fired brick.

Façade and door decorations are extremely simple but architecturally effective. The façades of the Capilla Real and Missions San Luis Rey and Santa Barbara and the side door of Mission San Buenaventura are neoclassic in their severity, yet they retain much of the older plateresque character. All they lack is the sculptured tracery that combined Gothic and Mudejar elements, and the fine details round door and window frames. These quasi-sculptured façade decorations appear somewhat unfinished. The total absence of decorative details strikingly enhances the structural rather than the organic aspect of the ornamentation. An example is the framed niche over the street-side entrance at Mission San Gabriel. But this neoclassic style, in which the disposition of the details of the Roman classic order suggests the sculptural, comes closest to perfection at Santa Barbara.

The richest ornament and that most Moorish in feeling is at Mission San Carlos. Over the entrance door, which is strongly neoclassic in every respect, is the relatively elaborate Mudejar window, a star-shaped opening designed from the combination of a circle and a square. The opening is framed by a series of moldings which, while repeating the design, splay outward and give it richness. The framing of the arched door with its concentric moldings again resembles the ancient Roman models, with moldings and panels on the entablature partly incised and partly in relief. There are two pyramidal finials at the bottom ends of the arches. More ornate is the interior doorway to the side chapel. Simple structures of classical proportions and with smooth columns that suggest the Doric frame a delicate Mudejar arch. The whole is typical of Spanish combination of styles; it is of excellent proportions, and the workmanship of the sculptured details is superior.

Because of the superior disposition of the carved details of the façade, the Capilla Real at Monterey, which has already been mentioned, is the best example of its type in the mission chain. More distinctive than the figure of the Virgin of Guadalupe which surmounts the façade are the architectural scrolls, moldings, and semiengaged finials that give to the whole an almost sculptured appearance. The work in stone is finer and more delicate than that in any of the missions. On each side of the arch is a small relief of branching and winding leaves, clearly the best and possibly the only remaining example of this type of ornamentation in a Franciscan church in California.

In contrast, the exterior of Mission Dolores is severely architectural, with no trace of sculpture as such. The interior, however, has perhaps the most elaborate original reredos of any of the missions. Here there is wood carving in the churrigueresque tradition but very much simplified, with niches for the polychromed figures. The reredos, however, cannot be classified as sculptural ornament since it was constructed of wood and, traditionally, was made in sections that probably had come to the mission from Mexico before 1810 when the neoclassic side altars which Engelhardt describes as "carved from wood and gilded" were installed.

Not to be overlooked are the sculptured decorations of the mission fountains. Of these only a few originals remain, but they are typical. The extant original fountains are those in the Peyri courtyard at San Luis Rey, at San Fernando, and at Santa Barbara. The largest is the double-tiered fountain at Santa Barbara. Here the stone bowls rest on volutes of the Ionic type and are channeled or grooved, with separating medallions. The carving is crude, like most similar work done by Indians. The Indians, however, worked from models. The topmost bowl is somewhat smaller than the other and has a globular spout rising above it, from which the water flows. The pedestal is of gray stone and rests in a large hexagonal catch basin. All the other mission fountains are of recent date and are either copies of those just mentioned or reconstructions from fragments discovered in the ruins. Almost all the carving or other decoration on the original fountains was architectural in character and was derived from source books. It is rather curious that there were no handsome fountains of the Mudejar type, the lower catch basins of which were similar in design to the choir window at Carmel. The only exception is the large fountain pond in the garden across from Mission San Fernando. In many missions the simpler fountains were built of ladrillos; there are several of this type at La Purísima Concepción.

The baptismal fountains also offer examples of carved decoration, although most of them were rather crude pedestals with a copper font in the hollowed-out top. The one at San Juan Capistrano was perhaps the most elaborate. It had twenty-seven Ionic flutes round the bowl part and an ornamental band of stems and leaves round the top. The pedestal was simple and rested on a square base; the bowl was a little more than three feet in diameter. The font at San Juan Bautista was shaped like a great narrow bell, with deep fluting on the side. It had a very short, round pedestal and rested on a square stone base. At San Buenaventura there are two small stone holy-water fonts, carved from dark-gray stone. They are embedded in the walls near the rear of the church and are marked by fairly deep fluting.

Other examples of carving can be mentioned, although they are not strictly decorative. The stonework in the form of a skull and crossbones embedded in the outer wall of the cemetery door at Mission Santa Barbara is very crudely done. The stone "gargoyles," or waterspouts, in the old lavanderías—though the ones at San Luis Rey do not properly belong to the architecture of that mission—are good examples of Indian carving. Heavy and massive, they have a pronounced primitive character and show no influence of traditional styles.

Not to be overlooked is the carving on the mission doors. Ordinarily this was extremely simple and usually consisted merely of a series of vertical wavy lines, generally parallel, that accentuated the height of the door. The design has often been called "The River of Life." It is found commonly on the heavy outer double doors of the church and the principal entrance to the convento. A particularly fine example is the side door at San Buenaventura. Other designs of "carved" wood on outer doors were as simple: some doors had an overlay of stained wood similar to heavy iron or bronze studding, with large circles at the intersections, others had only simple beveling on the heavy panels.

Some of the vigas also were carved, but the practice of carving them was not so common in California as in New Mexico. The corbels often had very interesting curved and stepped ends and offered a pleasing transition from ceiling to wall. One other form of decorative carving, although it is not strictly architectural, is found on some of the older pulpits and on altar railings and the balustrades of the choir lofts. The work was executed by the neophyte Indians from patterns supplied by the padres and the master carpenters. In Mission Santa Barbara the ceiling decorations in the form of rosettes, stars, and elaborate lighting motifs were carved from wood, painted in bright colors, and then attached to the ceiling. The designs were, as a rule, taken from books on classical architecture, but were often given local interpretations.

From the foregoing discussions of California mission architecture, it must be conceded that although the extant churches cannot compare in grandeur or beauty with some of the great buildings elsewhere in the world, they represent a form unparalleled in the history of architecture. It is an architecture of contradictions and even of anachronisms. It is at once original and eclectic; the structures appear to have grown from the very adobe from which they were made, and at the same time, with the simplicity born of restrictions, they reveal echoes of remembered glories. The padre-builders used the basic materials and adapted them to the buildings they established in a wilderness, for the heathen, and dedicated to the greater glory of God. In so doing they unwittingly established for posterity a style that has come to bear their name, Franciscan. In the last analysis it appears that motifs and style derivations, both of which can be arbitrarily assigned, are not very important. What is important is that, with but a few exceptions, the architecture and sculpture look right. Though at times the structures of the Franciscans may appear awkward and even crude, the decorations of their churches gaudy, and the details of form clumsy, virtually every church and even the minor buildings show that their builders followed the basic tenet of good architecture—form follows function. Perhaps no architectural style in history has created so much with so little; so much that is still ennobling with so little good material to work with; so much that is warm and touching in its beautiful simplicity with so little creative experience to fall back on. Perhaps more than anything else, the priceless intrinsic ingredient that the padres put into their buildings was the very one that prompted them to venture into the wilderness in the first place. That ingredient was Faith.

Founding Dates and Dimensions of the Missions

		Outside length of church building including sacristy at rear	Inside length of nave: entrance to reredos	Outside width of church	Inside width of nave at sanctuary	Height of walls at eaves	Height of gable or ridge pole	Height of tower(s) or campanario
San Diego de Alcalá	July 16, 1769	174.0	138.0	34.6	25.6	29.0	35.0	46.6
San Luis Rey de Francia	June 13, 1798	180.0(?) [f]	164.5	36.0	27.2	33.0	45.0	78.0
San Juan Capistrano	Nov. 1, 1776	180.0 [a]	146.0	30.0 [a]	27.5	Church and tower destroyed		
San Gabriel Arcángel	Sept. 8, 1771	172.0	142.2	35.0	26.5	30.0	34.0	Tower destroyed
San Fernando Rey de España	Sept. 8, 1797	163.9	153.9	37.0	25.0	26.5	32.7	Tower destroyed
San Buenaventura	Mar. 31, 1782	155.0 [b]	123.7	39.7	27.0	26.0	38.0	57.0
Santa Barbara	Dec. 4, 1786	179.0	162.5	38.0	27.5	29.9	43.0	70.7
Santa Inés	Sept. 17, 1804	163.0	137.5	36.7	24.7	26.0	36.0	44.3
La Purísima Concepción	Dec. 8, 1787	174.0	123.5	34.0	25.5	16.5	24.0	32.0
San Luis Obispo	Sept. 1, 1772	153.5 [c]	112.0	34.0	24.7	26.6	34.0	
San Miguel Arcángel	July 25, 1797	156.9	145.7	38.0	27.5	29.9	40.5	
San Antonio de Padua	July 14, 1771	200.0 [d]	148.5	40.0	27.5	26.0	32.0	40.0
Nuestra Señora de la Soledad	Oct. 9, 1791	67.6	46.3	24.6	18.3	14.0	17.6	
San Carlos Borromeo	June 3, 1770	167.3 [d]	150.0 [a]	39.0 [d]	29.0 [a]	26.0 [d]	35.0 [d]	61.0 [d]
Capilla Real, Monterey	June 3, 1770	137.3	131.7	26.6	20.3	22.0	32.0	36.6
San Juan Bautista	June 24, 1797	183.6	122.6	72.0	26.9 [e]	39.7	48.0	
Santa Cruz	Aug. 28, 1791		113.0 [f]		29.0	26.0	Church destroyed	
Santa Clara de Asís	Jan. 12, 1777		142.0 [f]		29.0		Church destroyed	
San José	June 11, 1797	123.7		30.25			Church destroyed	
San Francisco de Asís	Oct. 9, 1776	145.0	114.0	32.9	22.0	26.5 [g]	35.5	
San Rafael Arcángel	Dec. 14, 1817	88.0(?) [f]		42.0(?) [f]		18.0	Church destroyed	
San Francisco Solano	July 4, 1823	106.0 [h]	97.0	25.0	16.2	18.0	26.0	

Most of the measurements are taken from the Historic American Building Survey line drawings in the Library of Congress, Washington, D.C. Measurements are in feet.

[a] Measurements from Rexford Newcomb, *The Old Mission Chruches.*

[b] Includes base of the tower.

[c] Includes narthex and small sacristy back of sanctuary only.

[d] Measurements from Frances Rand Smith, *The Architectural History of Mission San Carlos Borromeo.*

[e] Width of present single nave; original width at sanctuary: 64.0.

[f] Measurements from Engelhardt.

[g] The floor slopes slightly upward; the roof line slopes downward from front to rear. Measurement is from near front of building.

[h] Measurements are of restored chapel.

READING LIST

BANCROFT, Hubert Howe. *California Pastoral, 1769–1848.* San Francisco, 1888. (Bancroft's *Works,* Vol. XXXIV.)

BEATTIE, George William. *California's Unbuilt Missions.* [Los Angeles: Privately printed, 1930.]

CARTER, Charles Franklin. *The Missions of Nueva California.* San Francisco: Whitaker and Ray, 1900.

ENGELHARDT, Zephyrin. *The Missions and Missionaries of California.* 4 vols. Santa Barbara, 1930. Also individual works by Engelhardt on selected missions.

HALLENBECK, Cleve. *Spanish Missions of the Old Southwest.* Garden City, N.Y.: Doubleday, Page, 1926.

JAMES, George Wharton. *In and Out of the Old Missions of California.* Boston: Little, Brown, 1905.

JUDSON, William L. "The Architecture of the Missions," in *Annual Publications of the Historical Society of Southern California, 1907–1908,* Vol. VII, Part II (Los Angeles, 1909), 114–118.

NEWCOMB, Rexford. *The Old Mission Churches and Historic Houses of California.* Philadelphia: Lippincott, 1925.

PALÓU, Fray Francisco. *Historical Memoirs of New California.* Edited by Herbert Eugene Bolton. 4 vols. Berkeley: University of California Press, 1926.

SMITH, Frances Rand. *The Architectural History of Mission San Carlos Borromeo, California.* Berkeley: California Historical Survey Commission, 1921.

WEBB, Edith Buckland. *Indian Life at the Old Missions.* Los Angeles: W. F. Lewis [1952].

QUOTATIONS

The quotation on page 16 is from Charles Franklin Carter, "Duhaut-Cilly's Account of California in the Years 1827–28," *California Historical Society Quarterly,* VIII, 160. That on page 20 is from George Vancouver, *A Voyage of Discovery to the North Pacific Ocean, and Round the World* (London, 1798), II, 35. The *informe* of 1787 mentioned on page 16, the annual report of Mission Santa Barbara dated December, 1796, mentioned on page 21, and the report of Mission San Buenaventura for 1808, mentioned on page 38, are in the archives of Mission Santa Barbara.

IV

The Existing Missions

MISSION SAN DIEGO DE ALCALÁ

First of the Alta California Missions, San Diego de Alcalá was founded on July 16, 1769, by Father Junípero Serra. Not far from the harbor of San Diego a simple *enramada* had been erected, the first "building" in California. The place seemed ideal: the soil was good, an arroyo supplied fresh water, and there were numerous Indian villages in the area. For months the founding party not only suffered extreme privation, hunger, and sickness but was harassed by Indians. The mission progressed slowly at first, and it never attained the prosperity of the others. Fernando Parrón and Francisco Gómez were its first pastors.

In 1774 the mission was moved to a site six miles farther inland, for the location near the Presidio had proved undesirable. At that time there was only a small church of adobe and wood, a small building for the padres, a few shops and storerooms, and some fourteen Indian dwellings. In an Indian attack in 1775 Father Luis Jaime was killed and the mission buildings were burned; within a year they were rebuilt. In 1780 a second, larger church was completed and the adjoining structures were enlarged. Tile was used for roofing after 1792. The mission prospered in spite of hardships; by 1797 it had a population of more than 1,400. Vineyards were planted and an irrigation system, barns, a tannery, shops, and granaries were built. The present church, begun in 1808, was completed in 1813.

After Mexico became independent in 1821, the provincial governors, the secularization laws, and the greed of the growing civilian population brought about the downfall of all the missions. Yet in 1832 San Diego still possessed large herds and flocks. After secularization, in 1834, San Diego was handed over to an administrator and the Indians were "freed." Pillaging and ruin followed. The first bishop of California, Francisco García Diego y Moreno, O.F.M., resided at San Diego in 1841 but found it so unsuitable that he soon moved to Santa Barbara.

Father Vicente Oliva was the last resident Franciscan at San Diego. In June, 1846, the Governor of California, Pío Pico, sold the mission buildings. American forces often occupied the mission in the next fifteen years, and some repairs were made. Finally, in May, 1862, the church and some twenty-two acres of land were restored to the Church.

Not until 1931 was a thorough restoration of the church building undertaken. After secularization it had gradually crumbled until only the façade and parts of the side walls remained. By no means a spectacular structure, its most interesting feature is the adjacent campanario with its five bells. The interior of the church has been renovated rather recently. A few statues dating from the mission period remain, and the relic room contains a few other historical objects. To the right of the entrance is the false-front façade, constructed as the outer wall of what was once the convento. Although services are held today in the mission church, the atmosphere of the whole is rather depressing.

The mission is some five miles east of U. S. Highway 101, in Mission Valley on the road to La Mesa (State Highway 90) just north of San Diego.

Mission San Diego de Alcalá   *The Doorway to the Church*

MISSION SAN DIEGO   *The Façade and the Campanario*

MISSION SAN DIEGO   *Entrance to the Garden*

MISSION SAN DIEGO   *The Campanario*

MISSION SAN LUIS REY DE FRANCIA

Founded June 13, 1798, by Father Fermín de Lasuén, one of the most beautiful missions, San Luis Rey, stands in a sheltered valley several miles from the ocean. This was Lasuén's ninth and last mission. Father Antonio Peyri was assigned to San Luis and served as its padre for more than thirty years, supervising the building program and the largest Indian population of the province.

The mission progressed rapidly and was prosperous from the very beginning. After the preliminary temporary structures were erected, plans for the extensive establishment were made. By 1802 an adobe church large enough for a thousand Indians had been completed. Construction of the quadrangle was as rapid: shops, various quarters, and storerooms were finished within another two years. Father Peyri, however, had more ambitious plans and in 1811 laid the foundations for the large church that is still in use. It was dedicated in October, 1815, but construction of chapels and adjacent structures went on for several years. The materials used were chiefly adobe faced with brick, and timbers (vigas) held in place by rawhide thongs. The quadrangle of the mission building was some five hundred feet square and covered about six acres. The long convento was faced with a corridor having thirty-two square pillars. There was a very large Indian village near the mission site which numbered 2,869 neophytes in 1826.

With Mexican independence came rumors of secularization, and to San Luis Rey this was especially disastrous. Discipline and community labor fell away; the buildings fell into disrepair. Peyri finally left, in 1832, and his going hastened the decline of the mission. Father José Antonio Anzar replaced Peyri, and Father Vicente Oliva of Mission San Diego took care of the temporalities in 1831 and 1832. In 1833 Pablo de la Portilla was appointed administrator, and even he with the help of Father Anzar was unable to control the neophytes who had been given their "freedom." In 1834 Father Bonaventura Fortuni turned over the mission to the administrators, Pío Pico and Pablo de la Portilla. Chaos ensued. The cattle were slaughtered for their hides; the lands were partitioned among the Indians and then stolen from them. In an attempt to stop the plunder, Governor Micheltorena returned the mission to Franciscan control in 1843, and Father Zalvidea took over. So little was left of lands and stock that the mission could not adequately feed and clothe the 400 remaining Indians. In 1846 Governor Pico sold the mission for $2,437. That same year Father Zalvidea died, the last successor of Father Peyri. During the Mexican War and for some time thereafter, United States troops were quartered in the mission; but in 1865 part of the mission property was restored to the Church by Abraham Lincoln.

In 1892 a group of Franciscans came from Zacatecas, Mexico, to take up residence, and in 1893 Father Joseph O'Keefe arrived at the mission with the intention of restoring it and making it a Franciscan missionary college. In the years between 1865 and 1892 virtually everything, including the altar, had been pillaged. After preliminary repairs, the church was rededicated in 1893. Since then, restoration has been extensive though gradual. Further improvements and the reconstruction of ruined buildings have almost completely restored the mission, and it has recaptured much of its early glory. It is now not only a parish church but an important part of the Franciscan apostolic college.

The mission church is unquestionably the most unusual of the chain. A large dome surmounts the crossing and there is a large octagonal mortuary chapel and a separate baptistery. The spaciousness of the whole is remarkable. The mission possesses an excellent collection of paintings and sculpture, most of which, although of the mission period, was brought from Zacatecas and elsewhere in Mexico after the restoration. The vestment collection is very large, and there are many fine examples of native Indian basketry.

The mission is in the village of San Luis Rey, five miles east of Oceanside, just off State Highway 76.

MISSION SAN LUIS REY DE FRANCIA   *The Mission Church*

82

MISSION SAN LUIS REY   *The Statues on the Façade*

MISSION SAN LUIS REY   *The Interior of the Church*

MISSION SAN LUIS REY   *The Stone Choir Steps in the Peyri Court*

MISSION SAN LUIS REY   *Statue of La Purísima Concepción*

MISSION SAN LUIS REY   *The Indian Stone Gargoyle*

MISSION SAN JUAN CAPISTRANO

The most romantic and most extensive of the ruined missions is San Juan Capistrano. The seventh mission to be founded, it was blessed on October 30, 1775, by Father Fermín de Lasuén, who was soon joined by Father Gregorio Amurrio. Scarcely had the settlement been established when news of the San Diego uprising reached the fathers, and the place was temporarily abandoned. A year later, Father Serra and Fathers Amurrio and Pablo de Mugártegui were present at the second founding, which took place on November 1, 1776. The next year the first section of the adobe church was finished; the small building is historically important, for it is the one in which Serra actually celebrated Mass and is the oldest building in California. Situated in a fertile valley with abundant water, the mission flourished, and soon the crops were more than sufficent for the needs of the community.

Although the little chapel was enlarged, it soon proved to be inadequate. Plans for a cruciform church, 146 by 28 feet, with a tower, bapistery, sacristy, and adjacent buildings, of quarried stone, were made by Fathers Vicente Fuster and Juan José Santiago. This church was to excel all others in the province; it was begun in February, 1797. Most of the work was under the direction of the master stonemason Isidoro Aguilar, but he died before the work was completed. The church, with adjoining convento and corridors, was nine years in the building.

The devastating earthquake of December, 1812, toppled the tall tower, rent the domes, and wrecked the church. It was never reconstructed, though the original adobe chapel was restored and somewhat enlarged for use as a church. At the time of the earthquake some 1,360 Indians were living at the mission.

During the Mexican period the mission gradually declined. In 1833 Governor Figueroa founded an Indian pueblo for the "emancipated" Indians, mission properties were turned over to white civilians, and the community was disrupted. Father Zalvidea remained as priest until 1842. Governor Pico sold the mission for $710.00 in 1845; in 1865 the decayed and neglected property was returned to the Church.

Attempts were made to preserve what remained of the stone church in the 1860's—the tottering domes were removed, gaps in walls were filled. A shingle roof placed over the ruins was blown off in a severe storm. After a long period of neglect, the Landmarks Club in 1896 began the work of preserving the various buildings. Father St. John O'Sullivan became resident pastor in 1910, and until his death in 1933 he worked incessantly to restore the ruined mission compound.

Several of the buildings facing on the patio have been restored and serve as museum rooms containing paintings, sculpture, vestments, and mission relics of various types. Three sides of the vast quadrangle are now enclosed; on the fourth side can be seen the foundations of the workshops. A parochial school, finished in 1928, occupies part of the north wall of the reconstructed area. Restoration of the original (the Serra) chapel was begun in 1922. Missing details were copied from patterns at San Luis Rey and Santa Inés. To replace the original altar, which had long since disappeared, a far more elaborate Spanish baroque reredos, with statues in the niches, was brought from Barcelona in 1906 and was installed in 1922–1924. It is 19 feet wide and 23 feet high. Paintings, statues, candelabra, and other furnishings in the style of the seventeenth and eighteenth centuries decorate both the sanctuary and the nave.

The gardens with their handsome fountains in Moorish style, the ivy-covered ruins, the beautiful setting in a small but very busy town, make San Juan Capistrano one of the most delightful missions to visit. It is in the center of the town of San Juan Capistrano on U. S. Highway 101.

MISSION SAN JUAN CAPISTRANO *Ruins of the Stone Church*

90

MISSION SAN JUAN CAPISTRANO   *The Campanario*

MISSION SAN JUAN CAPISTRANO *The Inner Corridor*

MISSION SAN JUAN CAPISTRANO   *Arched Entrance to a Corridor*

MISSION SAN JUAN CAPISTRANO   *Partly Restored Corridor*

94

MISSION SAN JUAN CAPISTRANO   *An Archway*

MISSION SAN GABRIEL ARCÁNGEL

The first Mass at Mission San Gabriel Arcángel was celebrated on September 8, 1771, in an enramada near what is now called the Rio Hondo. The mission was founded by Fathers Pedro Cambón and Angel Somera in a locality heavily populated by apparently friendly Indians. Within two years of the founding, more than 1,000 had been baptized, though the community grew slowly in the early years. Unruly soldiers stirred up the Indians and caused trouble for the padres, Antonio Cruzado and Antonio Paterna, who had replaced the founders.

When Father Lasuén became superior he moved the mission to its present site, in 1775. San Gabriel served as an important link between the west coast and the overland route from Sonora, and for some time it was a military center. Congestion at the mission was relieved when the pueblo of Los Angeles was founded. By 1784 San Gabriel had risen to first-rank importance in the province; its fields and herds were numerous, and it became the wealthiest of the missions.

The present church was begun in 1791. It was constructed partly of stone and brick and had a vaulted roof of concrete. The church was completed early in 1805, but the roof had to be replaced in 1807; the new one was of the conventional flat type covered with tiles. In 1812 an earthquake destroyed the campanario and many of the shops and severely damaged the church. An adobe granary served as temporary church until 1828, when the repairs were finally completed. From 1806 until 1826 Father José María Zalvidea controlled affairs. Under his direction the ranches were developed and the water-power system for the grist mill was installed.

After 1830 the usual political troubles affected San Gabriel; late in 1834 the mission was secularized and Father Tomás Esténaga turned over the inventory to the administrator. Little of value was left when the mission was returned to the Franciscans in 1843. In 1846 the mission was given by Pico to some Americans; the property was finally returned to the Church in 1859. The last Franciscans, Fathers Francisco Sánchez and José Jimeno, had left in 1852.

Until 1908, when the mission was entrusted to the Claretian Fathers, it was a parish church under the bishop of the diocese. Fortunately the interior of the church has been well preserved. Most of the other buildings have long since disappeared.

The mission today is a veritable museum. Of interest are the ancient cemetery, the partially restored ruins, and the handsome campanario that abuts the church building. In addition to a fine collection of vestments, silver, and other religious articles, there are excellent examples of colonial painting and sculpture in the church itself and in the adjacent museum rooms. The best-known works are the primitive

Stations of the Cross painted early in the century by a neophyte Indian—the most remarkable examples of such work in the missions. The reredos behind the main altar is in the typically classic style of the early nineteenth century.

The mission is in the city of San Gabriel, on Mission Drive, about ten miles east of the center of Los Angeles.

MISSION SAN GABRIEL ARCÁNGEL   *The Buttressed Wall of the Church*

MISSION SAN GABRIEL   *The Stairway to the Choir*

MISSION SAN GABRIEL   *The Campanario*

MISSION SAN GABRIEL   *The Side Portal*

MISSION SAN FERNANDO REY DE ESPAÑA

The last of the four missions founded in 1797, San Fernando Rey de España in the beautiful Encino Valley some twenty miles north and west of San Gabriel, was founded by Padre Presidente Lasuén on September 8. The soil of the valley was fertile, water was plentiful, and Indians were numerous in the vicinity. Fathers Francisco Xavier Uría and Francisco Dumetz were the first missionaries.

The mission was temporarily housed in a structure belonging to Francisco Reyes, alcalde of the Pueblo of Los Angeles. The usual construction program followed rapidly. One wing of the enclosure included a weaving room and various shops. Emphasis was on the crafts, in keeping with the aim to make the mission self-supporting. A second and larger church was finished and a second quadrangle wing was added—the adobe dwelling for the padres—in the second year of the mission's history. All the buildings were roofed with tile. By 1804 the mission counted nearly a thousand neophytes and an extensive Indian village of seventy houses with its own plaza was completed.

The permanent adobe church with its tiled roof and the adjacent compound were completed in 1806 and in December the church was dedicated. The entrance was on the west; the door had a round arch on the exterior and a flat lintel on the interior. The thick church walls permitted the use of shallow, recessed arches. Along the side walls there were nine of these arches, seven of them cut through for windows. The sacristy, behind the altar, was entered through a brick archway. This church was almost destroyed in the earthquake of 1812.

The extensive fields surrounding the mission were irrigated by means of dams and channels leading from an aqueduct. The mission soon became one of the thriving industrial centers of the area, supplying tallow, soap, hides, shoes, clothing, and numerous other articles not only to other missions but to presidios. From 1810 until the late 1840's, San Fernando was beset with trouble. During the chaotic Mexican period, Father Francisco Gonzalez de Ibarra held together the fortunes of the mission. In 1834 he turned over the properties to the civil administrator, Antonio del Valle. Deterioration commenced. When the mission was sold by Pico in 1846, Father Ordaz was the last Franciscan in residence. This sale was later declared invalid by the United States government. Not until 1902 were resident priests again sent to the mission.

San Fernando was intermittently used as the military headquarters of the California governors from 1833 until 1846; here also, Frémont made his headquarters in 1847. The distinguishing feature of San Fernando is the long building that is now the museum. After the church was abandoned, the largest room served as the mission chapel. By 1890 the church and most of the other buildings were almost totally ruined. The Landmarks Club undertook their restoration, and by 1897 much progress had been made. Subsequently, a good part of the long building and the church was restored. Part of the old plaza facing this building is now a public park separated from the mission by a highway. In it stands a large fountain, in the shape of the Moorish star, that originally formed part of the reservoir system.

Only a few examples of the original furnishings of San Fernando remain, but the halls and rooms are being refurbished with sculptures, paintings, and artifacts of the period. Cleaning and removal of overpainting have revealed mural decorations around doors and windows and along the dadoes—all Indian work executed under the supervision of the padres. The characteristic rawhide thongs fasten together the beams. Other features of interest are the vat and wine cellars, the smokehouse and kitchen, the massive substructures, and one of the longest extant corridors in all the missions.

The mission is about a mile and a half west of the city of San Fernando (off U. S. Highway 99), on Mission Drive near Sepulveda Boulevard.

Mission San Fernando Rey de España *Entrance to the Convento*

MISSION SAN FERNANDO REY   *The Long Corridor*

MISSION SAN FERNANDO REY   *Indian Decoration on a Corridor Arch*

MISSION SAN FERNANDO REY   *The Mission Kitchen*

MISSION SAN FERNANDO REY   *The Mission Fountain*

Mission San Fernando Rey *Statue of Father Serra in the Garden*
(modern)

MISSION SAN BUENAVENTURA

The founding of a mission on the Santa Barbara Channel had for thirteen years been one of Father Serra's most cherished ambitions. Finally, on Easter Sunday, March 31, 1782, he founded his ninth and last mission. The region was densely populated with Indians. They proved to be industrious, and the mission prospered in its fertile setting. San Buenaventura was one of the three missions and a presidio to be founded on the Santa Barbara Channel. When Serra went north to Carmel, Father Pedro Cambón was left in charge. Later, Fathers Francisco Dumetz and Vicente de Santa María were the pastors of the mission. By 1786 there was a fairly large Indian population.

Early in 1792 the first church was destroyed by fire; but a year later, when Vancouver visited the mission, a new church was already under construction. Very likely this was a temporary structure, for in 1795 the annual report by Presidente Lasuén mentioned that the masonry church was about half finished. By then three sides of the mission quadrangle had been completed. Workshops, a tannery, Indian quarters, and guest rooms were also built. Between 1804 and 1805, sixty-four individual adobe houses, with tile roofs, were built in the Indian village. While the church was under construction, a chapel called Santa Gertrudis was built for the Indian community at Casitas. This was used for worship after the earthquake of 1812.

The new church was completed on September 9, 1809, and in that year many of the best church furnishings were acquired. The 1812 earthquake almost destroyed the church, but by 1815 the reconstructed church was in good condition. By the end of 1816 more than 1,300 Indians and 30 white persons were living at the mission.

Although there was an Indian outbreak in May, 1819, it had no permanent effect on the growth of the mission. Building activities continued on a large scale; many houses were built for the Indians. Throughout California the mission workshops produced not only the food but soap, blankets, cloth, tools, and even weapons for the guards and the presidios. After 1812 the military became increasingly dependent on the missions and relations between the padres and the soldiers became strained.

After the 1820's San Buenaventura declined; the productive orchards, vineyards, and grainfields were lost to the new Mexican government. The mission was secularized in 1834. It became a parish church in 1842 but was temporarily restored to the padres in 1843. In 1845 Pico rented the mission for $1,630 a year. In June, 1846, he sold it for $12,000 to José Arnaz; the sale was subsequently declared illegal.

The "renovation" of the mission in 1893 was unfortunate. Windows were enlarged and the Indian decorations were covered with plaster and modern stencil work. The original tile floor, still in good condition, was covered with wood. In 1957 the interior of the church was restored, much of the restoration consisting of the removal of the earlier "modernization." The heavy ceiling vigas and the old tiled floor were cleared, and the wall decorations were restored and made as nearly like the originals as possible. The altar was returned to its original form and lowered to its former level. There are a few good pieces of colonial sculpture and a very fine set of Stations of the Cross in the church; the adjacent museum has fragments of fine old mission pieces.

Early in the twentieth century, modern business began to encroach on the former mission lands. The church now fronts the busy main street of Ventura; all that remains of the grounds is a small, lawn-covered enclosure. The church is near the western edge of the city, just east of U. S. Highway 101.

MISSION SAN BUENAVENTURA   *The Bell Tower*

MISSION SAN BUENAVENTURA   *The Side Entrance to the Church*

MISSION SANTA BARBARA VIRGEN Y MÁRTIR

On December 4, 1786, Mission Santa Barbara was founded—the first mission to be founded after Father Junípero Serra's death. It was consecrated by Father Fermín de Lasuén on December 16. Father Serra believed he had established this mission when he blessed the place that later became the site of the Santa Barbara Presidio chapel. Fathers Antonio Paterna and Cristóbal Oramas were the first missionaries assigned to the Santa Barbara Channel area, which was very thickly populated with Indians. The first church and convento were erected in 1787 (the second year). In 1789 a larger church of adobe with a tile roof was built; and a third, still larger one, was begun in 1783. This church served the growing community until it was destroyed in the 1812 earthquake.

In 1815 construction of the large stone church was begun, and five years later the building was completed. The design, which is almost strictly classical, was based on a book of Roman architecture. The church was planned by Father Antonio Ripoll. Because of its beautiful setting and graceful proportions, Santa Barbara came to be known as the Queen of the Missions. The church was 179 feet long and 38 feet wide; the 6-foot-thick walls were heavily buttressed. At first only one tower, that on the left, was completed (1820); the second was finished between 1831 and 1833. The beautiful new church was dedicated in 1820. There were also workrooms, living quarters, the Indian village, and an extensive water-works system.

The peace was broken by the famous Indian uprising that began at Santa Inés in February, 1824, and then spread to La Purísima and Santa Barbara. The northern missions had been taken over by the Zacatecan Franciscans in 1833. In 1834 Commissioner Anastasio Carrillo arrived to administer the mission properties. By 1839 only 246 neophytes were living at the mission. (In 1807 there had been more than 1,700 in the Indian village near the church.) However, Santa Barbara was established as the see of the first bishop of California, García Diego y Moreno, and when he died, in 1846, he was buried in the sanctuary of the mission church. That same year the mission was sold by Pico for $7,500 to Richard Den. A few Franciscans stayed on at the mission in quarters reserved for them; Father González Rubio remained for some thirty years, the last of the old missionaries.

A college for Franciscan novitiates was established in 1853 and was first housed in the mission, subsequently in the growing town. In 1856 it was reëstablished at the mission, where it has since remained as the major study house of the order. Throughout these years the buildings were always kept in repair. In 1865 some 283 acres were returned to mission ownership, and from then on, extensive alterations and enlargements were made. Among other things, a long, shingled roof on the convento was replaced by one of tile, and in 1905 an addition was made on the west end of that building.

In June, 1925, the mission was severely damaged by an earthquake; only the massive buttresses prevented the walls from buckling. The east tower collapsed, and the entire façade, together with the convento, was damaged almost beyond repair. The front of the church, the towers, and the convento were rebuilt exactly to the original specifications. Most of the interior was faithfully repainted; only the reredos back of the main altar was changed. The restoration was completed in 1927. Then, in 1950, it was discovered that disintegration of cement and of foundations was causing the church buildings to settle, and, as a result, the towers had begun to crack dangerously. The façade and towers were consequently demolished and the entire building front was reconstructed down to the subfoundations. When the restoration was completed, the church was rededicated on December 4, 1953.

Mission Santa Barbara is not only one of the architectural gems in the chain, but it is a museum of Spanish colonial sculpture and painting as well. The walls of the church are hung with typical examples of eighteenth-century Mexican paintings; the reredos has some fine examples of sculpture; and the museum rooms are filled with all types of religious and secular memorabilia of the mission period. The mission is today one of the most important archival centers for Franciscan, mission, and California history in the country.

The mission stands on high ground in the residential part of Santa Barbara, at the upper end of Laguna Street, four blocks north of State Street.

MISSION SANTA BARBARA   *The Church and the Moorish Fountain*

116

MISSION SANTA BARBARA   *The Neoclassic Portada*

MISSION SANTA BARBARA   *Door and Window in the Nave*

MISSION SANTA BARBARA   *The Front Corridor of the Convento*

Mission Santa Barbara   *Barred Door and Window of the Convento*

MISSION SANTA BARBARA   *The Stone Carving of the Lavandería*

MISSION SANTA INÉS VIRGEN Y MÁRTIR

The story of Mission Santa Inés has been a turbulent one almost from its beginnings. It was founded on September 17, 1804, by Father Estevan Tapis, as the last of the southern missions and the nineteenth in the chain. At the end of the year the first semipermanent adobe church and the convento, some 232 feet long, were built. The roofs of both were of poles covered with thatch. Between 1805 and 1812 many smaller buildings were constructed: shops, storerooms, a guardhouse, quarters for soldiers, and houses in the Indian village. All the buildings were of adobe and were whitewashed.

After the 1812 earthquake, between 1813 and 1817, a temporary church was hastily erected. The new church, about 25 feet wide and 138 feet long, with its adjoining campanario was built under the direction of Fathers Tapis and Uría and was dedicated on July 4, 1817. The walls are five to six feet thick and are heavily buttressed. The roof is of wood and tile. In the next several years the interior of the church was decorated and some additions and reconstructions were made.

A new era began for the missions in 1821, with the independence of Mexico from Spain. In 1824 the famous revolt of the Indians against the soldiers occurred; the storerooms and harness shops and the rear of the church were burned. The following year the reconstruction was completed. The decorations made at that time have endured, for the most part, to the present day. In 1834, in accordance with the secularization laws, the mission became a parish church, and in 1836 the mission was rented out. The first seminary in California was established at the mission by Bishop García Diego in 1843; it lasted until 1881. For two or three years after the end of the Franciscan period the mission was the victim of despoilers. Then, in 1846, the Americans took over, and in 1862 some of the properties were returned to the Church. The Franciscans had left the mission in 1850; from then on until the Capuchin Franciscans took over in 1924 there was a succession of both Order and secular priests.

The buildings virtually disintegrated in the last years of the nineteenth century, but no extensive repairs were made and no serious reconstruction was undertaken until Father Alexander Buckler's residence from 1904 to 1924. Major reconstruction and restoration took place in 1947–1948, and again in 1953–1954. Restoration has been slow and careful here and, on the whole, well done. There are excellent examples of colonial painting and sculpture, and a fine collection of old vestments in the church and the museum rooms. The reredos and sanctuary decorations comprise one of the few unrestored examples of colonial art in any of the California missions today.

The mission serves today as the parish church for the area. Beautifully situated in a lovely valley, it stands at the edge of the town of Solvang, some thirty-five miles from Santa Barbara on State Highway 180.

Even from the first, the name of the mission has been spelled in various ways. The form *Santa Inés* is the one now used, though by decision of the United States Geographic Board *Santa Ynez* is used for the mountains and other geographical features in the area.

MISSION SANTA INÉS   *The Convento and the Church*

Mission Santa Inés   *The Doorway to the Church*

Mission Santa Inés   *The Front Corridor*

MISSION SANTA INÉS *The Patio Garden*

MISSION SANTA INÉS   *The Campanario*

MISSION SANTA INÉS   *Corridor Adjoining the Patio*

MISSION LA PURÍSIMA CONCEPCIÓN

Mission La Purísima Concepción, the eleventh in the mission chain, was founded by Father Fermín de Lasuén on December 8, 1787. The site was in what is now the town of Lompoc, and the mission drew its neophytes from the dense population of Indians north and west of Santa Barbara. Fathers Vicente Fuster and José Arriota were the first resident missionaries. The first building of the new mission, a temporary structure, was begun in March, 1788. It was soon replaced by a large adobe church roofed with tile, construction of which probably began in 1801 and was completed in 1802 or 1803. With the convento and shops, most of which were also of adobe roofed with tile, this church was destroyed in the earthquakes of December, 1812.

A year later, construction was begun on a new mission at a site several miles northeast of the first. Father Mariano Payeras, who supervised the work, had a difficult task, for aid from the Pious Fund in Mexico had been almost totally cut off since the Hidalgo revolt in 1810. A residence for the padres was built in 1815, and by 1816 a long series of workrooms connected the residence with the church. The convento was unusually well constructed of brick and adobe. Besides the padres' quarters it contained rooms for guests, some shops, and a chapel. These faced a large double patio with corridors roofed with tile. Quarters for the Indians were also built. Before completion of the church in 1818, services were held in a "palisade" chapel and in the chapel of the convento. The campanario was added in 1821. There was an excellent water system with lavanderías and reservoirs. Much of this has been restored.

At one time more than a thousand Indians lived at La Purísima. In 1824 there occurred a serious Indian revolt that had its origin in the flogging of an Indian at Santa Inés. The revolt spread to Purísima and to Santa Barbara, and for nearly a month Purísima was in a state of siege.

Within ten years of its secularization in 1834, the mission was on the way to ruin. The church building collapsed in 1836. In 1845 the mission was sold to Juan Temple for $1,100, and thereafter the property passed from owner to owner. No attempt was made to keep up the buildings, and through neglect and vandalism they became completely ruined. The Church received some of the property back from the United States government in 1874 but soon sold it because of its dilapidated condition. In 1903 the Union Oil Company acquired the lands and in 1933 deeded them to Santa Barbara County. The State of California acquired the property in 1935. Restoration of the convento and workshops, as well as the church,

fountains, and several other minor buildings, was undertaken by the National Park
Service. The padres' residence was restored between 1935 and 1937 and the church
in 1941. The restoration on the whole is excellent. Several of the buildings now
serve as museums and house a fine collection of Indian material and an increasingly comprehensive collection of period sculpture and paintings.

The mission is just off State Highway 150 about four miles east of the city of
Lompoc. Lompoc is between Santa Barbara and Santa Maria, some nineteen
miles west of U. S. Highway 101 at Buellton.

MISSION LA PURÍSIMA CONCEPCIÓN   *The Fountain in the Olive Grove*

Mission La Purísima Concepción *The Convento*

Mission La Purísima Concepción   *Stone Piers at the End of the Convento*

Mission La Purísima Concepción *The Workshop Building*

Mission La Purísima Concepción   *The Campanario*

Mission La Purísima Concepción   *The Cemetery*

MISSION SAN LUIS OBISPO DE TOLOSA

On September 1, 1772, Father Junípero Serra dedicated the fifth mission in California to St. Louis, Bishop of Toulouse, at a site in a valley through which Gaspar de Portolá and Father Juan Crespi had passed in 1769 en route to find Monterey Bay and which had also been noticed by Captain Pedro Fages in the spring of 1772 when he was hunting bears. This place, La Cañada de los Osos (the valley of the bears), had seemed to Father Serra a suitable site for a mission. Here, in an area of friendly Indians, the customary *enramada* and the first temporary wooden buildings were erected. After Father Serra left for Monterey, Father José Cavaller was in sole charge of the mission, which he served until his death in 1798. The buildings were nearly destroyed in 1776 when hostile Indians set fire to the tule-thatched roofs. Subsequently the inflammable roofs were replaced by roofs covered with tiles.

The mission was prosperous and by 1805 had several ranches, one with an asistencia, Santa Margarita; but at no time was it very populous. Much of its success was due to the energetic Father Luis Martínez, who had come to San Luis Obispo on the death of Father Cavaller.

The church that still stands was built of adobe between 1792 and 1794, although the church front with its belfry-like façade was not completed until about 1820. Next to the mission quadrangle were two rows of tile-roofed adobe houses comprising the Indian village. Behind the quadrangle were storage tanks, tanning vats, a large reservoir, and a grist mill. Another mill, the second grist mill in California, of Mexican style and powered by water, had been constructed in 1798.

After reaching its peak as an agricultural center in 1818, the mission rapidly declined. It was secularized in 1835. The last Franciscan resident at the mission was Father Ramón Abella, who left in 1841. In 1844 the Indians were given their freedom, the mission was made a pueblo, and the church became a public building. The following year Governor Pico sold the mission for $510. However, the new owners were dispossessed the next summer and in 1859 the mission compound, with its adjacent orchard and vineyard, was returned to the Church by the United States government. The mission had become a parish church soon after its secularization and still serves as one. The adobe walls were covered with wood, a wooden steeple was placed on the roof of the old convento, the cloisters were boarded up, and the mission roof was covered with shingles.

Despite the encroachment of a modern city virtually to the doors of the church, some characteristics of the original building have been retained. True restoration

of the remaining buildings, the church and the old convento, was begun in 1933
by Father John Harnett. He restored the former portico, took down the bell tower,
and replaced the bells (which had come from Peru) in their original setting. He
did not, however, restore the wall with an arched gate which originally stood in
front of the church portico. The façade is unlike those of the other missions in
that it sets back from the right end of the convento.

The rather plain, neoclassical reredos in the church has several good late
eighteenth-century sculptures. A typical baroque Concepción stands on a bracket
on one side, and there is a fine polychrome statue of St. Anthony in a side chapel.
The Stations of the Cross and several other paintings are well worth attention and
study. The doors are very massive and are paneled and beveled and studded with
spikes. Adjacent to the church on the left is the partially restored convento (complete restoration will never be possible). In it there are several museum rooms
containing characteristic eighteenth- and nineteenth-century religious and secular
objects, including the old mission registers signed by Serra and some especially fine
vestments.

San Luis Obispo is one of the eight missions which because of their favorable
situation became the nucleus of flourishing communities after California was ad-
mitted to the Union. It is in the center of the city of San Luis Obispo, a few
blocks west of the main shopping center.

MISSION SAN LUIS OBISPO DE TOLOSA   *The Façade and the Convento*

MISSION SAN LUIS OBISPO   *The Main Door to the Chapel*

MISSION SAN MIGUEL ARCÁNGEL

Mission San Miguel Arcángel was founded July 25, 1797, by Presidente Fermín de Lasuén as the sixteenth mission in the ever-lengthening chain. Fathers Buenaventura Sitjar and Antonio Horra were assigned to the new establishment. The new venture began auspiciously; by 1806 there were nearly a thousand Indians at the mission. In the years 1799 to 1804 the first temporary buildings had been replaced by adobe structures. In 1806 a fire destroyed part of the church and the greater part of the storerooms and workshops.

During the height of its progress the mission was a community of neophyte craftsmen and the center for all types of agriculture. Between 1806 and 1820 there was continuous building activity, and the living quarters, workshops, and storerooms were constantly being expanded, not only at the mission itself but at its widespread ranchos. In 1816 the stone foundations for the large adobe church were laid. Father Francisco Martín supervised the construction of this building. It was completed in 1818. The decoration, finished in 1821, includes the finest mural work in the mission chain.

After the tumultuous revolutionary troubles in Mexico, the mission was forced to contribute all manner of goods to the support of the military and their families. Attempts were made as early as 1831 to confiscate the properties, but secularization was delayed until 1834. The last Franciscan padre to reside at the mission until its return to the Order in 1928 was Father Ramón Abella. He had remained at the mission because there was no replacement for him; when he died in 1842 only thirty Indians were living there. Administration of the mission had been given to Ignacio Coronel in 1836. There was much changing of both priests and administrators between 1834 and 1842, when the Franciscans ceded the mission to the first bishop of California. By that time the buildings were very much run down. In October, 1845, the properties were confiscated by Governor Pico and sold. Between 1842 and 1878 the mission had no resident priest.

The mission buildings, together with some adjacent lands, were returned to the Church in 1859. But until 1878 the convento and other buildings were occupied as residences, saloons, or shops, but little was done to prevent their deterioration. The first restoration of the convento was made between 1886 and 1889 by the Reverend Joseph Mut. He is the only priest buried in the cemetery. The main buildings were first renovated in 1901.

Since the Franciscans returned to San Miguel in 1928 the quadrangle buildings have been almost completely restored. Those which formerly housed the shops and storerooms are now used as living quarters and classrooms, for the mission is a branch school for the training of priests. The convento houses a museum containing an excellent collection of memorabilia of the late mission period, as well as fine vestments and paintings. The church itself is a museum of late Spanish colonial art. The grounds and the surrounding area have been similarly restored, and across the highway can be seen the ruins of the once extensive Indian village. San Miguel now serves as a parish church. It is situated in the village of San Miguel on the old U. S. Highway 101, about nine miles north of the city of Paso Robles.

MISSION SAN MIGUEL ARCÁNGEL   *Gateway to the Compound*

MISSION SAN MIGUEL   *The Church Façade*

MISSION SAN MIGUEL   *The Front Corridor*

MISSION SAN MIGUEL   *The Restored Fountain*

MISSION SAN MIGUEL   *Enclosure Gate*

MISSION SAN MIGUEL   *Fountain in the Garden*

MISSION SAN ANTONIO DE PADUA

The setting of San Antonio de Padua in a small fertile valley between high mountains has remained almost unchanged since the day of its founding. Established on July 14, 1771, San Antonio was Father Serra's third mission. The usual pole stockade enclosed the primitive wooden chapel and other buildings. However, in 1773, Fathers Miguel Pieras and Buenaventura Sitjar, the padres in charge, moved the mission to a site farther up the valley where water was more abundant. By the end of the year an adobe church, workshops, and dwellings were completed. The mission soon prospered; crops were abundant. A new adobe church, 133 feet long and roofed with tile, was built in 1779–1780, the first tile-roofed building in the province and, according to reports, the finest in the country. A large Indian dwelling was also built at this time. By 1806 the community had numerous other buildings as well as a water-powered mill, and the Indian population numbered nearly 1,300.

In 1810 the present church was begun. It was completed in 1813 and the long convento with its fine corridor was finished the following year. The large quadrangle was rebuilt: new quarters, workshops, walls, storage areas—all strongly constructed of adobe or brick and most of them roofed with tile.

After Mexico became independent in 1821, San Antonio, like all the other missions, declined, for financial support was intermittent. In spite of droughts, and sickness among the Indians, construction continued. By 1828 there was a network of walls, buildings, corrals, and irrigation ditches surrounding the church. The irrigation system developed by Father Sitjar—twenty miles of ditches and troughs in a canyon behind the mission—was a marvel of engineering. Yet by 1833 the Indian population had dwindled to 587.

After secularization of the missions in 1835, Mission San Antonio fell into ruin. It was confiscated by the Mexican government, but in 1843 it was temporarily returned to the Franciscans. The last resident Franciscan, Father José Gutiérrez, left in 1844. The properties had deteriorated to such an extent that Pico was unable to sell them, as he had those of the other missions. Then, in July, 1846, the United States government took protective custory. A small part of the property was returned to the Church in May, 1862.

An attempt was made by Father Doroteo Ambris, sometime after 1848, to preserve the buildings. After his death in 1882, they were completely neglected until in 1903 the Historic Landmarks Committee of the Native Sons of the Golden West undertook to preserve the ruins. These were further damaged in the earthquake of 1906. In 1928 the property was returned to the Franciscan Order. The work of complete restoration was undertaken in 1948. The church and the adjoining convento were rebuilt. Most of the ruined buildings are gradually being restored and the large quadrangle is again taking form. The church was rededicated in 1950. The establishment is now a novitiate for the Franciscan Order.

The enclosed entry of the church has a vaulted ceiling, and the ceiling of the church itself is not the usual flat one (see p. 57). San Luis Rey, Santa Barbara, San Miguel, and Carmel missions have contributed paintings, statues, and ecclesiastical objects to refurbish the interior.

The mission is in an isolated valley three miles from Jolon, on the Hunter Liggett Military Reservation, seventeen miles southwest of King City and twenty-three miles northwest of Bradley, both of which are on U. S. Highway 101.

MISSION SAN ANTONIO DE PADUA   *The Façade and the Convento*

MISSION SAN ANTONIO *The Campanario and the Cross*

MISSION SAN ANTONIO   *The Campanario*

MISSION SAN ANTONIO   *The Museum*

MISSION NUESTRA SEÑORA DE LA SOLEDAD

Plans for the establishment of the mission known as Soledad were made as early as 1789. Several missions were asked to contribute goods, cattle, and provisions to the founding, and Fathers Diego García and Mariano Rubí were appointed the first pastors. The mission was founded by Father Lasuén on October 9, 1791, on the site called Chuttusgelis by the Indians. Plans for buildings were drawn and vineyards, orchards, and irrigation ditches were soon laid out. Under the direction of the padres, the Indians worked in the fields and vineyards, made adobe bricks, and constructed storehouses, living quarters for the priests, and a church. This church, of adobe and roofed with straw, was completed by 1797. But progress, both material and spiritual, was very slow, for the region was sparsely settled. The Indian population of the mission at its peak, in 1805, was only 688.

Mission Soledad was constantly beset with troubles: Indian unrest, epidemics, the unhealthfulness of the locality, the unhappiness of the missionaries. But in 1805 the church was enlarged and for a time the mission prospered.

Governor José Joaquín de Arrillaga died at Mission Soledad in 1814 and was buried in the church. And when Father Florencio Ibañez died in 1818 from overwork and illness after fifteen years of duty at the mission, he too was buried there.

When the notorious pirate Hippolyte Bouchard raided the coast in 1818, most of the refugees from the coast missions fled inland to Mission Soledad.

In 1828 the prefect of the missions, Father Vicente Sarría, took over the duties at Soledad, for it was too difficult to obtain a missionary. Sarría was the last Franciscan resident there. Exhausted from work, worried by threats of secularization, and almost starving, the old priest died in May, 1835. No one succeeded him, for Soledad had been united with San Antonio under the secularization decree of 1834.

The buildings at Soledad were never extensive. The few that did exist were of adobe, and the heavy winter rains caused them to be in constant need of repair. In 1831 the church collapsed. A small chapel built soon afterward is the structure that has recently been restored. After Sarría's death, the abandoned mission continued to shelter a few Indians. In 1846 Pío Pico sold the near ruin for $800.

Until 1954 no attempt was ever made to restore the mission, even after the property was returned to the Church. The little chapel has now been restored and is adequately furnished with pictures and a few statues. It is surrounded by fields, and adjacent to it are the mounds and crumbling walls of the former mission buildings. It is on a country road branching from U. S. Highway 101, three miles south of the town of Soledad, and is a mile west of the highway.

Mission Nuestra Señora de la Soledad   *Ruins of the Buildings*

MISSION SOLEDAD   *The Restored Campanario*

MISSION SAN CARLOS BORROMEO

On June 3, 1770, Father Junípero Serra founded the second of the California missions, San Carlos Borromeo, at the Presidio of Monterey. The next year he moved it to the valley of the Carmel River, five miles from the presidio. Officially the new church was called Mission San Carlos de Monterey, but it has been variously called Carmelo, San Carlos de Carmel, San Carlos Borromeo del Carmelo, and Carmel Mission. Serra made this mission his headquarters and from it directed the administration of the expanding mission system.

The first structures were temporary: dwellings, storerooms, corrals for stock, and a guardhouse, in addition to the wooden church. In 1774 adobe construction was well under way. An adobe church built under the direction of Serra himself, and in which he was buried when he died in 1784, served for some twenty years. In 1793 the present stone church was begun under the supervision of Father Lasuén, the master mason Manuel Estevan Ruíz having been brought up from Mexico for the work. It was dedicated in September, 1797, with Lasuén, the *padre presidente*, officiating. In 1882 the graves of Presidentes Serra and Lasuén and Fathers Crespi and López were discovered within the church. Father Serra's remains now rest in the beautiful sarcophagus (of recent design, by Jo Mora) illustrated here.

Although it was the administrative headquarters for the California missions, Carmel never had as many Indians as the others; the highest number was 876, in 1795. Lasuén's successor as presidente, Estevan Tapis, moved his headquarters to Santa Barbara.

Between 1818 and 1833 Carmel Mission was sorely beset. Much sickness and many deaths, as well as depredations by the military, hastened its decline. It was secularized in 1834 and turned over to a commissioner. By 1836 the church was almost completely destroyed. For a time services at Carmel were held by the resident priest from Monterey. When Governor Micheltorena returned the mission to the Franciscans in 1843, only ruins remained. The roof of the church collapsed in 1852, and for some thirty years the building remained uncovered.

After 1870 Father Angelo Casanova, the parish priest at Monterey, determined to restore the buildings. In 1884 the church was reroofed and rededicated. Later a steep-pitched roof was put on it, which protected the building but marred its appearance. Little more was done until 1924. Since then a program of construction, started by Father Ramón Mestres, has been under way. The work has been careful and the restoration successful, especially since 1933, when Carmel became a separate parish church.

A tile roof put on the church in 1936 has restored its original appearance. Most of the padres' rooms in one wing have been restored and now serve as a museum. Here are the old refectory, the kitchen, and, in another part of the building, Father Serra's cell. The first library in California is housed here. The soldiers' quarters, restored in 1942, now serve as a rectory. The chapel of the Blessed Sacrament was at one time the dining room for the Indians. A parish school building erected in 1945 occupies the site of the dormitories for Indian children. Restoration of the mission compound is almost complete.

Religious paintings and sculpture of excellent quality, some of which originally belonged to the church and the convento, have been returned to the mission. There is a fine collection of vestments and other articles used during the mission period, and other furnishings date from that and the early American period.

Certainly Carmel Mission, with its rich brown sandstone bare of any covering stucco, its tower with a Moorish dome, its windows, and its setting against the sea and the mountains, is as beautiful as any mission. Although the church is not large, it is nonetheless monumental, and it has great architectural interest. The small garden with its fountain and flowers in niches is one of the handsomest in the mission chain.

Mission San Carlos is on the southern edge of the city of Carmel, in the Carmel Valley, just off State Highway 1.

MISSION SAN CARLOS BORROMEO (CARMEL) *The Façade of the Church*

162

Mission San Carlos Borromeo   *The Bell Tower*

MISSION SAN CARLOS BORROMEO   *The Doorway to the Church*

MISSION SAN CARLOS BORROMEO   *Rear View of the Church*

MISSION SAN CARLOS BORROMEO *Chapel with the Serra Sarcophagus*
(modern)

MISSION SAN CARLOS BORROMEO *Detail of the Serra Sarcophagus*
(modern)

MISSION SAN CARLOS BORROMEO   *The Old Kitchen*

MISSION SAN CARLOS BORROMEO *The Mission Cemetery*

THE CAPILLA REAL, MONTEREY *The Façade*

THE CAPILLA REAL, MONTEREY   *Door to the Transept*

MISSION SAN JUAN BAUTISTA

Mission San Juan Bautista in its lovely setting remains virtually as it was when the first temporary structures were dedicated on June 24, 1797. The fifteenth mission in California, it was blessed by Father Lasuén. Its progress was extremely rapid, for within a year an adobe church and numerous dwellings had been completed, and by 1800 there were nearly six hundred Indian converts. A larger church was planned, and in 1803 the cornerstone of the new building was laid. However, Father Felipe Arroyo de la Cuesta arrived in 1808 and, having more ambitious plans, proceeded to build a large three-aisled church to accommodate 1,000 Indians. Its walls were of adobe, and its roof was of tile. The church was dedicated in June, 1812, by Father Estevan Tapis, who had become presidente on the death of Father Lasuén. The expected large congregation did not materialize. For this reason, and probably also to prevent earthquake damage, the two side aisles were closed off by filling in the arches. The decoration of the large reredos was the work of Thomas Doak, the first American settler in the province.

The mission achieved its greatest population and affluence in 1823 under the leadership of Fathers Arroyo de la Cuesta and Estevan Tapis. Father Tapis came to San Juan Bautista in 1812; he died in 1825 and was buried in the church. He was especially successful in the teaching of music to the Indians. Father Arroyo de la Cuesta compiled a scholarly dictionary and index of Indian phrases. He remained at the mission for twenty-five years, until 1833.

San Juan Bautista was secularized in 1835, and José Tiburcio Castro was made major-domo. He had some trouble with the Indians and some conflicts with the padres, but on the whole settled the affairs of the mission promptly and well.

The mission church was regularly provided with pastors, for by 1839 a small community had grown up near the mission. In 1861 a school and orphanage was opened, which continued in operation until 1906, when the earthquake severely damaged the buildings.

In 1865 Father Ciprian Rubio erected an unsightly wooden bell tower some two and a half stories high. During restoration of the buildings after the earthquake of 1906 and in subsequent years many of the "improvements" of the previous period were removed. Except for reroofing, bracing of the walls, and improving of the grounds, there has been little restoration. The original outer walls of the church remain only in part; in several places they have been shored up by concrete buttresses on the outside. The front corridor, 270 feet long, with its fine row of arches, is in excellent condition.

The mission owns a fine collection of paintings of the apostles, as well as Stations of the Cross. The museum, now in the convento, displays typical mission church articles and materials collected in the early American period.

The mission is now a diocesan parish church. It is in the center of the village of San Juan Bautista, which lies four miles south of U. S. Highway 101, some seventeen miles north of Salinas. Near the highway leading to San Juan is a twentieth-century replica of the bell tower at the Pala Asistencia. This attractive embellishment to the highway is illustrated on page 182.

MISSION SAN JUAN BAUTISTA   *The Convento Corridor*

MISSION SAN JUAN BAUTISTA   *The Bell Window*

Mission San Juan Bautista   *The Simple Campanario*

MISSION SAN JUAN BAUTISTA   *Mission Gate and Arches*

Mission San Juan Bautista   *Entrance to the Sacristy*

MISSION SAN JUAN BAUTISTA   *Moorish Arch in the Ruins*

MISSION SAN JUAN BAUTISTA   *The Baptistery*

MISSION SAN JUAN BAUTISTA   *The Reredos*

Mission San Juan Bautista   *The Mission Bell*

MISSION SAN JUAN BAUTISTA   *Highway Marker* (replica of bell tower at Pala)

MISSION SAN FRANCISCO DE ASÍS

Mission San Francisco, better known as Mission Dolores, is the only mission dedicated to the founder of the Franciscan Order. As early as 1770 the viceroy of New Spain, the Marqués de Croix, had proposed its establishment, but it was not actually founded until October 9, 1776. Father Francisco Palóu officiated at the founding. The site, which had been selected by Juan Bautista de Anza, was near a pond which Anza in March had named Laguna de los Dolores for Our Lady of Sorrows.

Palóu began construction of a permanent church early in 1782, which was finished by his successor, Father Pedro Benito Cambón, in 1791. This undoubtedly was not an imposing structure. The present church, which was begun in 1792, seems to have been completed by 1810, and within the year the interior decorations were finished and two gilded side altars installed.

The mission never attained the wealth and prominence of some of the others, although the Indians wove cloth and made pottery there. Several factors prevented its rapid growth: the Indians were prone to run away; the sandy soil offered little opportunity for agriculture; and frequent epidemics decimated the population. The cold and foggy climate finally prompted the founding of an asistencia across the channel to the north at San Rafael, in 1817, and Mission San Francisco Solano at Sonoma, in 1823. Many of the neophytes from Dolores were removed to these establishments.

In September, 1834, Mission Dolores was secularized and the property was transferred to Commissioner José Estudillo. At the time, there were twenty-seven buildings besides the monastery and the church. The mission became an Indian pueblo. By 1841 the structures were in ruins, and services in the church were intermittent. Franciscan authority ceased in 1845.

In July, 1846, Captain John B. Montgomery took possession of the San Francisco region for the United States. During the gold rush years the mission structures, except the church, were used as rooming houses, taverns, and even as a dance hall and a brewery. A new St. Francis parish, with secular clergy, was formed, which used church equipment from Mission Dolores. In 1853 the priest started a school near the mission church and a seminary in the old monastery. In recent years the church has been used only occasionally for services.

Some attempt to preserve the crumbling church building was made in the 1860's when Father Prendergast covered the adobe walls with boards. Windows were cut into the south wall of the nave; the old altar was covered with a new white one.

In 1916 effective restoration of the church, which had survived the 1906 earthquake, was begun by the Reverend John Sullivan. The weakened roof and walls were reinforced by concealed steel beams. Some redecoration of the walls was made; but the original ceiling decorations painted by the Indians and the churrigueresque reredos were left untouched. These and some of the wall decorations are perhaps the most attractive features of the mission. The two neoclassic side altars, which with their polychromed wooden statues were installed by Father Abella in 1810, are in good condition.

Nothing remains of the quadrangle buildings, and the adjacent cemetery has been carefully relandscaped. The rather unpretentious and very individual façade is so hemmed in by its city environment that it appears far less imposing than it really is. But even without its adjacent convento, and without its gardens and trees, the old building somehow has maintained its character.

The mission is in the central part of the city of San Francisco near the intersection of Sixteenth and Dolores streets.

MISSION SAN FRANCISCO DE ASÍS (DOLORES)   *The Façade*

MISSION DOLORES   *The Reredos*

MISSION SAN FRANCISCO SOLANO

To the northeast of Mission San Rafael, in a valley north of San Pablo Bay, the last of the missions was founded, on July 4, 1823. It was dedicated to St. Francis Solanus by Father José Altimira.

The original plan had been to abandon Mission Dolores because of the poor climate, and to found a new mission and transfer the San Francisco and San Rafael neophytes to it. Some controversy, however, arose, and a compromise was reached by founding the new mission without abandoning either Dolores or San Rafael.

Sonoma Mission, as it is more commonly known, had a very brief history. Founded after the establishment of the independence of Mexico, it was small and simple and never attained the stature of a major mission.

The church of adobe and wood was dedicated in April, 1824. It measured 105 by 24 feet and was probably similar in appearance to San Miguel or Santa Inés. Within a year Altimira constructed the long convento and, at its rear, workshops and quarters for the guard. In 1826 a band of Indians burned the buildings and drove Father Altimira to San Rafael. From that time until secularization there was a succession of priests, none of whom could properly control the natives. The most influential man in the area, the *comandante*, Mariano Guadalupe Vallejo, alone was able to exert some control. He kept the church in repair, made some improvements, and added a hideous square tower. In the eleven-year existence of the mission, the largest population and greatest wealth was in 1832 and 1833.

After secularization in 1834, the buildings fell into disrepair and by 1843 were almost in ruins. The present "church" was actually a chapel constructed between 1840 and 1843. Plans were formulated by Pico in 1845 to sell or rent the mission, or what remained of it. In 1846 came the Bear Flag revolt. After the occupation of California by the Americans, parcels of the original mission lands were returned to the Church, but the buildings were seldom used. However, in 1881 the mission was sold by the bishop, and the chapel and the convento were used as storehouses until they almost disintegrated. Attempts at restoration began in 1903, when the California Historical Landmarks League acquired the property. Several years later the mission became a state monument.

The extant chapel is some 36 feet long and about 16 feet wide; it is the smallest of the existing "church" buildings. To the right of the chapel is the partly restored convento, about 95 feet long. In this the ceilings are of rough planks resting on unhewn vigas, very much like those in some of the pueblo churches in New Mexico. Formerly a layer of tules (bulrushes) covered the planks, and the tile roofs rested on these. The convento had a covered corridor both in front and at the back, the one at the back facing the quadrangle (which no longer exists). The tiled roof of the corridor was supported by redwood posts rather than by the usual brick or stone pillars with arches.

For years this chapel and the adjoining building were used as a museum of heterogeneous Californiana. Until recently little was done to preserve the structures; temporary wooden roofs and brick were used to preserve them when they were in private hands. Except for the starkly simple chapel and its adjacent building there is little of interest at this mission. It seems anomalous that for the last mission in the chain the simplest, most primitive, and unpretentious construction methods and materials were used. Construction at the end of the mission period was simple as at its beginning.

Mission San Francisco Solano is near the plaza in the town of Sonoma, some forty-five miles northeast of San Francisco.

189

MISSION SAN FRANCISCO SOLANO (SONOMA)   *The Mission Bell*

MISSION SAN FRANCISCO SOLANO (SONOMA)   *The Chapel Doorway*

V

Missions That Time Has Destroyed

MISSION SANTA CRUZ

Like Mission Soledad, Mission Santa Cruz seemed fated to be unsuccessful. Although built in a pleasant coastal valley, near a river, it was some distance from El Camino Real. On August 28, 1791, Father Fermín de Lasuén consecrated the site. With Fathers Alonso Salazar and Baldomero López present, and with help from the San Francisco Presidio and the Indians, the building was soon under way. The formal founding took place on September 25. In February, 1793, a new church was started on higher ground. The foundations of this church were of heavy stone, the front wall of masonry, and the roof of timbers and tile. The church was dedicated in May, 1794. The resident padres were Fathers José Antonio Sánchez and Luis Gil y Taboada. Several workshops and storerooms were built and within a year the quadrangle was almost complete.

Nevertheless, the Indian population at Santa Cruz did not increase, and by 1796 there were only about five hundred Indians living there. Desertions were common. The mission was plagued with troubles. A heavy rainstorm so severely damaged the church in the winter of 1799 that it had to be rebuilt. There was a shortage of workers. Then, in July, 1797, Branciforte, the third California pueblo, was established near the mission by Governor Diego de Borica. Its presence was not conducive to the success of the mission, for friction developed between the rowdy settlers and the Indians on one side and the padres and neophytes on the other. Taking advantage of the confusion at the time of Bouchard's raid, the white settlers almost stripped the mission. In the first decade of the nineteenth century, American adventurers began arriving, as well as traders from foreign vessels putting in at Santa Cruz. With a depleted Indian population, Santa Cruz was ready for secularization as early as 1805. In 1832 the mission was turned over to the Zacatecan Franciscans; two years later, in August, it was turned over to an administrator and it became a curacy. The Indians were given their freedom. The former mission properties were dispersed through land grants; by 1839 only seventy Indians remained at the mission.

In 1840 the church tower was demolished by an earthquake. Father Real, who had moved to the community, was the last Franciscan there. Pico could not even sell the Santa Cruz mission; indeed, there was little to sell. A series of earthquakes in January, 1857, leveled the old church.

In 1931 a replica of the mission church, somewhat smaller than the original, was constructed on a site not far from where the original mission had stood. It is a very simple church with an arched doorway, a three-story tower to the right, and a short one-story building, suggesting the convento, to the left. The tile-roofed corridor is supported by wooden posts. The church contains a few examples of mission sculpture and painting. It is near the center of the city of Santa Cruz, on Monterey Bay, about seventy miles south of San Francisco.

MISSION SAN JOSÉ

On June 11, 1797, Mission San José was founded by Father Lasuén on the eastern shore of lower San Francisco Bay for the purpose of making contact with the numerous Indians of that area. A few days later, Fathers Agustín Merino and Isidoro Barcenilla, with a number of soldiers, began the work of building a chapel and temporary shelters. For some time, few conversions were made, for the Indians in the vicinity were generally hostile.

Although the mission was virtually a punitive center for subduing marauders and apostate neophytes, a program of extensive construction was begun in 1806 with the building of a new church, which was finished three years later. The tower was never completed, however, because earthquakes were common in those years. Mission San José never attained any architectural distinction; it remained a very simple structure. A daguerreotype made in 1852 or 1853 shows a flight of steps leading to the front entrance, which had a small sculptured portico, somewhat like a miniature temple front, flat against the wall. Apparently there was a long building adjoining the north wall of the church in the manner of a lean-to. All the buildings appear to have been roofed with tile.

Fathers Buenaventura Fortuni and Narciso Durán had come in 1806, and the two served the mission extraordinarily well. Under Father Durán's direction, Mission San José reached its highest population of some 1,800 Indians in 1831, at the very time the mission system was beginning to decline. Like San Juan Bautista, it became famous for its music.

After the independence of Mexico, replacements of priests from Spain were no longer permitted by the government. In 1833 Father Durán, who was also presidente of the missions, ceded San José to the Mexican Franciscans from Zacatecas. Father José Rubio took charge of the mission, and it, like Mission Santa Clara, retained its prosperity for a remarkably long time. It was the last to be secularized. In 1836 Father Rubio turned over the mission to an administrator, and by 1839 it was in very poor condition. By the time San José was temporarily returned to the Franciscans in 1843, it had suffered from pillage; three years later, Pío Pico sold the property to his brother Andrés for $12,000. In 1858 this sale was nullified and the church building, together with some twenty-eight acres, reverted to the Church. The following year some attempts were made to rebuild and modernize the old church, but an earthquake in 1868 caused the building to collapse, for the buttresses had been removed. A new wooden church of French design was constructed on the old tiled floor. In the 1880's a seminary was built on adjacent mission property; later a Dominican orphanage occupied the site. Only one building from the mission period survives—a part of the old convento. In 1916–1917 this was restored and repaired to some extent, and it now serves as a museum.

The mission is directly on the old East Bay Highway about fifteen miles northwest of San Jose, on the road to Niles.

MISSION SANTA CLARA

Mission Santa Clara was founded by Father Tomás de la Peña on January 12, 1777, on the banks of the Guadalupe River. At first the mission did not prosper, for the Indians were not attracted in any number. The padres had difficulty in securing laborers for construction and farm work. Additional troubles came from the neighboring pueblo; the colonizing scheme of the government proved to be a nuisance to the missions. In 1781, because the river repeatedly flooded the church, Mission Santa Clara was moved to a new location on higher ground and the new church building was begun. It was completed and was dedicated by Father Serra in May, 1784, soon after the death of its founder, Father José Antonio Murguía.

With the opening of this new and elaborate church, a period of great prosperity set in; the land was unusually productive and there was a large Indian population. About the year 1800 there were more than 1,200 resident Indians, and by 1827–1828 the population numbered almost 1,500. The church and the other mission buildings were enlarged in 1795. However, in 1812 and again in 1818, the church was so severely damaged by earthquakes that another site was selected. The third church was dedicated in August, 1822.

Father José Noboa succeeded Father Murguía. In 1794 Father Magín Catalá came to Santa Clara and for years was a guiding force; he and the equally energetic Father José Viader were responsible for the success of the mission and for the pretentious new church.

Because of the new laws in Mexico after the revolution of 1821, the Spanish Franciscans were forced to cede their posts to Zacatecans who were of Mexican birth. In 1833 Father García Diego, who in 1840 became the first bishop of California, took over the mission. In December, 1836, the mission was secularized; within three years most of the property and livestock had disappeared.

The Santa Clara–San José district figured prominently in the political and religious affairs of the province. The priests had charge of the entire northern area for several years, and they had many dealings with the pueblos and the fluctuating government. Yet the mission steadily declined; by 1844 there were only 130 neophytes. When the United States government took over, some of the sales were declared illegal, and in 1864 some of the property was returned to the Church.

In the meantime, with the American occupation the need arose for English-speaking priests, and the bishop ceded Santa Clara to the Jesuit Order with the stipulation that a college be established. In 1862 the old church was renovated, the façade was completely rebuilt, and the crumbling adobe tower was replaced by two towers, one on each side. By 1885 complete renovation of the church was necessary. The old murals were ruined beyond restoration; however, a fairly successful transfer of the ceiling decorations was made to the new church.

After a series of fires in 1909, 1913, and 1926—the last totally destroying the church—the mission church was rebuilt in 1929. Little of the original structure remains, though a few relics, statues, and paintings have survived. The church is now in the center of the University of Santa Clara campus, serving as both a college chapel and a parish church. In the library-museum there is an extensive collection of mission books, artifacts, paintings, and other religious objects.

MISSION SAN RAFAEL ARCÁNGEL

When San Rafael was founded on December 14, 1817, it was established as an asistencia, or branch, of Mission Dolores. The intention was to provide a place where sick Indians could recuperate. Father Luis Gil, who had considerable medical knowledge, was made guardian. Within a year the mission population included many converted heathen in addition to the Indians transferred from Dolores, and by 1821 San Rafael had nearly seven hundred Indians. Father Gil built an adobe church about 88 feet long and 42 feet wide, with walls about 18 feet high. It was one of the smallest and simplest, architecturally, of the mission churches. Besides the chapel there were living quarters for the padre and hospital rooms for the sick. Two star-shaped windows, one above the other, relieved the plainness of the façade. Since there was neither campanario nor tower, a primitive crossbeam on posts was used for hanging the bell.

Subsequently additions were made, resulting in an L-shaped building. The quadrangle was never completed. Mission San Rafael was of little importance except as a deterrent to the Russians, who were attempting to colonize the area a scant hundred miles to the north. Most of its success must be attributed to Father Juan Amorós, who took charge in 1819. He resisted the abandonment of the asistencia. Finally, in 1823, the establishment attained independent status, and the next year it contributed a number of neophytes to the founding of the last mission, San Francisco Solano. Mission San Rafael continued to grow and had a population of some 1,100 by 1828. Notwithstanding its progress, the mission had continual trouble with the Indians. After Father Amorós' death, in 1832, there was a good deal of conflict between the new padre and the Indians, as well as with Mariano Guadalupe Vallejo, comandante of the northern frontier.

Secularization came rapidly to the small mission. In 1834 it was made a parish but was united with both Mission Dolores and the Sonoma mission. The administrator turned Mission San Rafael into an Indian pueblo and distributed the properties. By 1842 the mission was abandoned. Governor Pico sold the property for $8,000 in 1846; however, this sale was later declared invalid, and six and a half acres of land were returned to Church ownership in 1855. Services were held in St. Vincent's Orphanage north of San Rafael, for the mission church was almost beyond repair. Finally, in 1870 the ruins of the mission were cleared away to permit construction of a parish church. Recently, a replica of the old mission has been erected near the original site.